Confidentiality and Clergy: Churches, Ethics, and the Law

William W. Rankin

MOREHOUSE PUBLISHING
Harrisburg, PA • Wilton, CT

Morehouse Publishing
Editorial Office
78 Danbury Road
Wilton, CT 06897

Corporate Office
P.O. Box 1321
Harrisburg, PA 17105

Library of Congress Cataloging-in-Publication Data

Rankin, William W., 1941-
  Confidentiality and clergy: churches, ethics, and the law/
William W. Rankin,
    p.   cm.
  Includes bibliographical references.
  ISBN: 0-8192-1530-9
  1. Clergy—Professional ethics. 2 Episcopal Church—Clergy—
Professional ethics. 3. Anglican Communion—Clergy—Professional
ethics. 4. Confidential communications—Clergy. 5. Pastoral
theology. 6. Pastoral theology—Episcopal Church. I. Title.
BV4011.5.R35   1990   90-37966
241.641—dc20   CIP

Printed in the United States of America
by
BSC LITHO
Harrisburg, PA 17105

To Robert Coles

Contents

Acknowledgments

Much of the writing for this project was done at the College of Preachers, in Washington, D.C., where I was given a fellowship in 1988. The Reverend Canon Charles J. Minifie is the president of the college, and I convey my sincerest thanks to him and his staff for their support.

Some of this material was presented as a lecture at the Duke University Divinity School, and some was presented at a meeting of the Virginia Episcopal Clergy Association in 1988. I am indebted to my great friend Professor Harmon Smith and to Dr. Joe Mann of Duke and to the Right Reverend Peter Lee, Episcopal bishop of Virginia. I presented some of this material in 1989 to the clergy conference of the Diocese of California. I express my thanks to the Right Reverend William E. Swing, bishop of California, for that opportunity and for all his warm support.

A number of people have read early drafts of these chapters and offered very helpful suggestions. These include Professor Harmon Smith of Duke; Professor Owen Thomas of the Episcopal Divinity School; Professor Louis Weil of the Church Divinity School of the Pacific; and Dr. John Archer, now of Berkeley, California. For the friendship and scholarly competence of these folks I am profoundly grateful. None of them is responsible for any shortcomings in the final product.

I have received much assistance in diverse ways from Bill Ibershoff, Ed Thomson, Ivan Weinberg, Ken Johnson, and Bill Rodiger, all attorneys. None of them is responsible for any mistakes I might have made regarding the law. Much help in writing has come from Anne Lamott. She knows how grateful I am for her assistance and her friendship. William Swing, John Burt, John Coburn, and Edmond Browning have been very supportive of me, each in his unique and fine way. My profound thanks to them.

My "buddies in the trenches" at St. Stephen's Church ought to be mentioned. During the crazy time of our litigation, we

vii

learned a new twist to the petition "Save us from the time of trial." These were the people especially available to help: Kitty Lehman, Amelia Wilcox, Marjorie Moore, Al Haag, Carla Hansen, Dorothy Jones, Sandra Ogden, Valerie Bishop, Bill Cannady, Dan King, Charles Gibbs, Charles Wilson, Carl Mosher, Bill Englebright, Peter and Marne Kellogg, and Bob Kane. What a fantastic group. Also I thank, for their friendship and support, the Reverend Dr. George Regas of Pasadena; the Reverend Dr. David Ames, OSD, of Brown University; the very Reverend Bruce Jacobson of Burlington, Vermont; and Dr. Martha Price of Indiana University.

Ted McConnell of Morehouse Publishing must surely be one of the best editors in the business. He has also been a dear friend over many years.

To Sally, Amy, Rob, Fred, Lois, and Bob I convey heartfelt thanks for the support and affection down the years.

William Rankin

Introduction

Clergy belong to a professional class marked by certain character-istic duties. One of these is the duty to retain confidences. The clergy's unique role and function in human interaction includes the premise that confidence-keeping is expected and must be upheld. Clergy assuredly could not fulfill their roles rightly if they did not respect people and privacy. A clergy person who breached confidentiality would soon be mistrusted and eventually ignored, if not positively resented, by those among whom he or she ministered. Honoring confidences is therefore crucial to the clergy's role; we would find it difficult to imagine a ministry of integrity where a clergy person departed from the confidentiality duty even slightly.

To be a trusted, principled, honorable person means, however, that sooner or later clergy may become privy to sensitive information that will result in a crisis of conscience: There may arise a strong impulse to divulge information learned in confidence. A moral quandary can then occur in which a duty to keep a confidence comes into conflict with a duty to divulge. Much support could perhaps be adduced for each duty, yet a decision, says the conscience, must be made. (Indeed, not to decide is to decide.) The reasons a clergy person could give for divulging or not divulging might come from various church authorities—the Bible, church history, consultation with superiors, with profes-sional colleagues, perhaps with attorneys also. But in the end, one decides for one's self. I have discovered that the great reservoir of church teaching and thinking on confidentiality may be difficult to find when it is needed most; once found, it can seem largely irrelevant and even arcane. I have learned also that much of what can be found from church sources needs to be supplemented by a thorough review of the applicable law, diligently sought from the best available legal counsel.

The need to have a focused resource on the ethics and law of confidentiality for the clergy was once urgent in my life, and I became very aware that such a resource did not exist. I have written this book out of my own need, and so it concentrates upon the Episcopal Church's tradition, at least in a few of its chapters. But I presume to say that the book as a whole might be useful to non–Episcopal Church people, too—both because it may partly fill a gap in the literature of other denominations and because the general ethics, law, and applications chapters are broader than merely "Episcopal" in scope.

While researching this project, I found myself looking at the professional codes of doctors, lawyers, and others. I was concerned by what these had to say about confidentiality and how they had come to understand it as an aspect of a professional ethic. I was particularly concerned by how these codes rationalized divulgence of a confidence, since divulgence is the hard choice, the choice that must vigorously be justified. It struck me that there is no generally recognized code of professional conduct for Christian clergy. Nor is there among the churches a broadly supported doctrine, principle, or even premise upon which a theory of confidentiality might be based. The Episcopal Church in particular has no authoritative professional code of ethics for its clergy; nor does it have a clear confidentiality guideline for either its clergy or its laity. The Episcopal Church has tended to avoid doctrinal rigidity—and rightly so, in my view. There is, thus, partly by default I suspect, a zone of silence around the subject area of professional ethics for clergy and around the confidentiality issue in particular. I do not lament the absence of dogmas or codes in the Episcopal Church. Indeed, I believe the strength of our church lies in its possessing a certain flexible openness to experience, a commendable respect for the exigencies of unique times, places, and individual circumstances.

On the other hand, both clergy and laity may be placed at an unnecessary disadvantage owing to a lack of clarity concerning professional ethics in general and the confidentiality issue in particular.[1] Whether or not clergy and churches are becoming increasingly vulnerable to litigation, the lack of a code means that it may be useful to draw together some ideas here about confidentiality—both to provide an initial resource for others and to stimulate further research and debate. I do not claim any other achievements for this book. Certainly I do not claim to offer anything "definitive." I would be pleased if what has been begun here should be of help to others. I would be delighted if the church, perhaps churches, is stimulated to go further than I have.

I am not entirely certain what a confidentiality statement should look like within a professional code of clergy ethics. I do not know whether such a thing would end up being more stultifying than helpful. I note, however, that physicians, nurses, attorneys, and counselors of various sorts have codes and that most of these contain confidentiality provisions. I am not sure how helpful in practice these are to all the various professionals for whom they are written. Most of these codes express what we already know, which is that we should generally keep confidences but that in exceptional circumstances we have a duty to divulge.

It is very clear that complex issues and dilemmas concerning confidentiality do arise for clergy with great frequency and in many different contexts. There are apparently countless varieties of human need. Surely these cannot all be anticipated in a rule book. Yet one supposes that it *is* possible to discover a sense of the game concerning what to do with confidential communications. The present book is intended to convey such a sense. It cannot offer a simple, legalistic solution to the general problems that may arise around the issue of confidentiality, especially within the frequently mysterious and ambiguous context of faithfulness to God and service to God's people.

A note concerning a few terms. I have used such various terms for clergy as *pastor, priest, clergy person,* and the like and such other terms as *priest-penitent, pastor-communicant,* and the like to signify a particular category of confidential communications. The different single and dual terms are each interchangeable: A Lutheran pastor, for example, is sufficiently like an Episcopalian priest to justify my use of either term, and a priest-penitent privilege in one state statute is comparable to a pastor-communicant privilege within the laws of another state.

The scope of this book cuts across the fields of theology, ethics, church history, pastoral theology, and law—the reader will discover that I believe clergy can learn from other professions' thinking and experience. I have no doubt that there are *many* in each of these fields whose competence far exceeds mine in several respects. I have tried to be faithful to the scholarly interests of seminary students and faculty but also faithful to the needs and experiences of parish clergy as well. In the last chapter I have tried to be faithful to my own experiences without being either self-indulgent or overly whimsical.

The first chapter is concerned with the different roles of clergy within the ordinary parish context. The various "hats" clergy can wear, even in the one job of being a pastor, incline them toward different ethical and practical considerations and behaviors. The different tasks that clergy must assume within their one role as pastor may have different implications for how they handle confidentiality.

In the second chapter we will look at the confessional situation and trace the understanding of what it is, and isn't, through the history of the Church of England. The "seal of confession" is a stringent way to protect confidentiality in the clergy-penitent context. An examination of the development of "seal" thinking is helpful for understanding what exactly the obligations of Episcopal clergy might be in a confessional situation. The Episcopal situation is compared with, and contrasted to, that of the Church of England in chapter 3.

In the fourth chapter the duty to keep a confidence is considered in tension with the duty to divulge, the duty to care, and other duties (such as protecting the life, health, and welfare of certain others). In chapter 5, the previous chapter's thinking is extended to areas where particular circumstances might conspire to make even an initial inclination to honor a confidence inappropriate or moot.

Chapter 6 contains an examination of professional ethics, law, and role morality as they relate to the issue of confidentiality. Since confidentiality is such a crucial matter for lawyers, the legal profession has a highly developed professional code. So I have used the field of legal ethics to examine confidentiality from a professional ethics point of view. This chapter also includes a presentation of the major legal issues pertaining to the priest-penitent privilege. The various states have accorded clergy, or at least "penitents," a legal privilege not to divulge in testimony what has been disclosed to clergy in bona fide counseling or confessional situations. We will explore what this actually means to clergy facing a subpoena to give testimony.

The final chapter entails helpful (I hope) hints about what should be done if a clergy person and/or a church congregation become involved in litigation and the public scrutiny that frequently accompanies it. The suggestions made here are based upon my own experience. Though I hope the situation will not arise for others, what was developed in my own parish may end up being consulted by others in a moment of similar need.

After completing the research and writing for this project, I have finally come to the unsurprising conclusion that there is no guaranteed way of making the right, or safe, decision every time. I have concluded also that despite the sometimes convoluted intricacies of theology, ethics, and law, we all tend to do right and good when we are basically intelligent, caring, respectful, and considerate of other people. I am quite overjoyed, in fact, to have arrived at this point.

1

The Ethos of the Church and the Ethics of Its Clergy

Many years ago, in the infamous late 1960s, when the world seemed to be coming apart for many Americans, a gifted educator spoke to some church people about the function of the church in society and the role of its clergy. Against a social background of disillusionment and cynicism regarding racism and militarism, this man said that churches should be beacons of moral, intellectual, and spiritual purity. He said that the churches and their clergy should "shine with the purity of a gemstone."

Though this exhortation may be overly simplified, the power and the beauty of the idea cling. Despite our recognition that moral rigor is difficult to sustain for long, there is yet a capacity in us to value what this educator was attempting to say. Something in us acknowledges that he was, and is, correct.

We do expect churches to be communities of people sincerely striving to respond to the spirit of Jesus—even though we recognize that hypocrisy and self-serving occur in all people and institutions. We do expect clergy, those "called" to a particular ministry of service to Christ and Christ's community, the Church, to make sincere attempts to live consistently within the spirit of Jesus—even though we recognize that none is perfect. To expect that Christian communities and ordained individuals will seek conscientiously to form themselves in accordance with a particular spirit (the spirit of Christ) is, in fact, to take these institutions and people at their word. Insofar as a church and its clergy diligently try to form themselves in a Christ-like spirit, we can speak of their integrity and authenticity; and thus we commend them.

The Chinese educator Lin Yutang once wrote "Why I Came Back to Christianity," an article originally published in *Presbyterian Life*.[1] In this oft-reprinted piece he stated his great respect for the "clarity and simplicity" with which Jesus disclosed both God's knowledge and God's love. Lin Yutang celebrated his own return to the Church, for the Church, he said, proclaims a "higher life" and a "higher level" upon which conscientious people are

1

called to live. The Church is where one goes who has "a yearning for spiritual values." It is a community for those who can "be moved to unselfish sacrifice." He offered a description of Christian life: "That higher life concerned with spiritual values and conscious of the mysteries of the moral law within and the starry heavens above is the 'life plus.' "[2] To be sure, we are not, as churchgoers, *better* than anyone else; rather, we recognize something urgent about both the possibility of "life plus" and the possibility of failing to claim it. As Lin wrote so succinctly,

I believe we go to church not because we are sinners, and not because we are paragons of Christian virtue, but because we are conscious of our spiritual heritage, aware of our higher nature and equally conscious of our human failings and of the slough of self-complacency into which, without help from this greater power outside ourselves, we so easily fall back.[3]

From his point of view, the Church and the clergy are here, among other reasons, to support and reinforce our "higher nature," the best that is in us as identified by Christ's own life. Indeed, a decidedly unfortunate condition would arise if the Church and its clergy ended up supporting and reinforcing human failings—repeated behavior not consistent with the spirit of Christ.

What Lin Yutang had to say about the Church, the clergy, and our higher nature bears directly upon the organization and administration of a church institution, its policies, practices, and procedures—and the professional ethics, formal or implicit, of the church's clergy. These should be designed to support and reinforce our higher nature. By the same token, the structure and practices of the Church, and the ethics of its clergy, should enable the recognition, diagnosis, and treatment of human failings—not, to be sure, from the vantage point of moral superiority but out of respect for the ways healthy institutional and corporate life promotes individual well-being, and vice versa.

The testimony of church and business people alike is ample and forceful: Good institutional leadership entails open and clear lines of authority, responsibility, accountability, and communication. It requires clear definition in terms of an institution's overall mission and the organizational practices supporting the same. With any institution of no matter what size, the integrity and authenticity of its functioning depend chiefly upon the moral qualities of its constituents and particularly upon those of its leadership. In the Church especially, it is difficult to have a sound institution, morally speaking, if the clergy do not hold themselves

2

accountable to their own highest nature. An accounting along this line can be made by means of the study and practice of professional ethics.

Professional Ethics in the Church

Certain organized forms of expertise have been described by the term *professional.* Members of the clergy are generally regarded as members of a profession, and it is usually held that in their work they are responding to a transcendent purpose, which they experience as a "calling." This means that they are embarked upon an endeavor different from, say, earning a living or "making money."

As a class, professionals usually must undertake advanced education and training. They generally cultivate certain specialized skills that are applied in working with other people whose problems or needs require a specialized human interaction. Frequently professionals are expected to make decisions affecting the health and/or welfare of other people, drawing upon their uniquely focused knowledge or experience.

If a question should arise concerning the approach, behavior, or consequences of this professional service, it is generally supposed that only another professional in the same field can render a valid judgment. If, for instance, a question arises about a particular brain surgery, people reasonably assume that review by a brain surgeon would be more suitable than would a review by a priest. If, however, a question arose concerning a priest's performance of a sacramental rite, we would expect a more valid judgment from another priest, rather than from a brain surgeon.

For the most part, professionals may only be evaluated appropriately by those within the same profession. The overall ethos of the given profession presents the context within which the norms and standards of that profession are articulated. These norms and standards themselves, and their supporting rationales, constitute the ethics of the profession. Within the churches, different denominations have fashioned different statements concerning professional ethics. In those denominations where there is no statement, it is possible nonetheless to establish such an ethic, at least minimally, by inference. It seems reasonable, for example, to suppose that clergy in any denomination would, and should, be expected to cleave to certain norms as a matter of principle, even if they occasionally depart from these. The duty to tell the truth, keep confidences, keep promises, treat people with respect, treat them fairly, and so on would be among these norms.

Clifton Fadiman offers us a useful anecdote. The rector of a parish of which the late nineteenth-century financial and business genuis Jay Gould was a member had somehow saved around $30,000. The rector asked Gould how the money could be invested to greatest advantage. Gould advised purchasing Missouri Pacific stock, but he did so "in strictest confidence." The stock rose, as predicted, but it eventually plummeted spectacularly. The rector then complained to Gould, who returned the original $30,000 and added $10,000 more. At this moment the rector, whether from guilt or joy at his rescue, admitted to Gould that he had shared Gould's strictly confidential tip with several others in the congregation. Gould replied, "They were the ones I was after."[4]

We laugh. Yet once Gould's craftiness has been appreciated, the image of the rector lingers disquietingly. Why? He is, once we think about it, the fool in the story; actually he is a harmful fool. Being in the ethos of the Church—indeed, being accountable as a professional—is the rector's job. But the rector betrayed a confidence and, moreover, was known by Gould to be inclined in that direction. For the trick to work, Gould had to be able to predict the rector's behavior. Although Gould gained personally, a number of others lost. These were, in fact, made victims— certainly by their own opportunism, also by Gould and, unwittingly, by the rector. Gould "won." The parishioners who invested, lost. Most of all, however, the rector lost, for he is revealed to be naive and, in the present circumstance, harmful. The whole force of the anecdote turns upon his violating a confidence, and upon Gould's being able successfully to *predict* that violation. In the end, what is given to church people in the humor of this anecdote is diminished by our uneasiness over the rector—his overall lack of credibility and competence as a professional. One imagines the rector as similar to the woman in Joseph Conrad's "The Return" who "strode like a grenadier, was strong and upright like an obelisk, had a beautiful face, a candid brow, pure eyes, and not a thought of her own in her head."[5]

What clergy, and lay people, are instead called to do as stewards of Christ's Church is to align the Church as much as possible with Christ's spirit. This includes, one thinks, a spirit of truth, honesty, integrity, and authenticity. That there is so much inside each one of us, and in the culture surrounding us, that seduces us away from these commitments should only make more important our consciousness of our Christian vocation to protect and serve the Church in a Christian way. The urgency of this is brought out by Kirkpatrick Sale in a clever way. He wrote of a mythical kingdom where the entire food supply had mysteriously become contaminated, so that anyone consuming it would become crazy. The leadership in that kingdom was confronted with the tragic choice of allowing the populace to starve or of feeding them and making them insane. Luckily there was a small bit of grain left over from the previous year. The decision was made to feed the populace the poisoned food so they would not starve. But the decision also included this: "We must at the same time keep a few people apart and feed them on an unpoisoned diet of the grain from previous years. That way there will at least be a few among us who will remember that the rest of us are insane."[6]

Much in the Christian heritage supports the notion that the world, with all its blandishments, tendencies to meanness, self-serving craziness, and the like, is analogous to the insane populace in Sale's story. (The world is not, of course, to be written off on that account; it is, however, to be seen for what it is, at least in part). The people eating the unpoisoned grain (the "true bread," conceivably) are the Church—at least the Church when it is choosing to take in the good grain. The clergy's highest duty, within the context of Sale's story, is to ensure that the Church gets the good grain. Therefore, it is important that clergy themselves not get confused or indifferent concerning their task.

A potential check upon tendencies of this sort is a code of professional ethics. Surely codes, by themselves, do not good professionals make. But they can help. Key elements of a code of professional ethics for clergy could include some of the moral principles to be discussed further in this book.

Professional Ethics and Personal Virtue

With or without formal codes, clergy should be *willing* to take seriously the importance of professional ethics. But as history suggests, such a willingness should not at all be taken for granted. Fraudulent and self-serving practices are not unique to those few TV evangelists who recently have been publicly disgraced. Objective evidence suggests, moreover, that "ecclesiastical crime" is a serious and widespread phenomenon. One cannot say

5

for sure that the perpetrators of ecclesiastical crime are clergy, of course. One *can* reasonably suppose, though, that diligence on the part of clergy could significantly reduce the magnitude of such crime. Martin E. Marty recently reported in the *Christian Century* some statistics by David B. Barrett's *World Christian Encyclopedia:*

Barrett estimates that such practices as skimming, pilfering or embezzlement amounted to $300,000 around the world in 1900, had risen to $5,000,000 in 1970, $30,000,000 in 1980 and now—hold on to your hats!—$650,000,000 this year (1988). . . . And there is little reason for optimism. The computers and those who program them expect $2,000,000,000 in churchly crime in the year 2000.[7]

One does not, of course, encourage clergy or congregational lay leaders to become police investigators; that is not consistent with the affirmative spirit of Christ. Yet, there are indications of, well, negligence, which call into question the willingness of church leaders, clergy and lay alike, to be the diligent stewards we are all called to be. We have to be *willing* to operate at the highest levels of institutional and professional stewardship. This requires an effort, for the things that threaten and undermine institutional integrity are rarely easy to discover. As Nobel laureate Joseph Brodsky once told a college graduating class, "Such is the structure of life that what we regard as Evil is capable of a fairly ubiquitous presence if only because it tends to appear in the guise of good. You never see it crossing your threshold announcing itself: 'Hi, I'm Evil!' "[8]

All this moves the discussion to the importance of discrimination in discernment. To be faithful to the highest in us, to be the best possible stewards of Christ's community, we should recognize all the major, relevant aspects of situations presenting themselves to us, and we should characterize them appropriately. Otherwise our decisions, our judgments, will be inadequate at best and hurtful at worst. In comic novelist Joseph Heller's book *God Knows,*[9] the narrator, King David, insists that when Solomon decided to cut the famous baby in half to show his fairness, he was dead serious—he meant to go through with it because, as Heller maintains, he was an idiot. He was not being ironic; he was not testing the integrity of the two women who wanted custody—he actually thought it was a good idea, a solution. Solomon was unable to perceive what was essential in the situation, a complex situation requiring a discerning analysis— an ability, at any rate, to treat a baby as a precious thing rather than, say, as a loaf of bread.

Somewhat less humorously, but equally an instance of mis-perceiving the situation, is an event involving a bishop of the Episcopal Church several years ago. In general outline, the bishop, an ex officio trustee of the diocese, was approached by a lay trustee of the diocese, who asked to make his confession. The confession was centered on an admission by the trustee that he had taken several thousands of dollars in negotiable securities from diocesan funds to bolster some of his personal investments. Upon hearing this confession, the bishop counseled that the other trustees be notified of the affair. This, however, apparently prompted the man's reminder to the bishop that the confession is always confidential and that if the matter should come to light the man would kill himself.

The situation then took a problematic turn. The bishop, apparently deciding the situation required a "pastoral" response, attempted to work with the perpetrator to replace the missing funds, all the while covering up the fact of the embezzlement. Together the bishop and his confessant took additional diocesan funds to effect a hasty "into and out of" the market on an alleged sure thing. Not surprisingly, this money was lost as well. The cover was blown off shortly thereafter by the sudden death of the confessant. The bishop was eventually indicted, tried, and convicted of criminal negligence. He served five years in a state prison, and the diocese was severely damaged for years after.

One supposes that this bishop was not the first ordained person, nor the last, to misread a situation, and then on the basis of the misreading, to commit himself to a disastrous direction. There is a fairly recognizable and predictable failing here. Clergy are too frequently inclined to see themselves as pastors first and as careful administrators distantly second, if at all. Many of them enter seminary with pastoring as the highest priority, and many base their entire professional careers upon pastoring. There is surely no doubt either that the bishop in question had definite pastoral responsibilities to the perpetrator. But for all that, the "hook" that enables clergy to be manipulated and turned in dangerous directions is frequently their inclination, born of their need to "pastor," to misread situations confronting them. If we see ourselves—more, *want* to see ourselves—as pastors only, we will always be vulnerable in circumstances requiring something more and different from us. The bishop in this story evidently saw himself only as a pastor. Thus, he failed to accept his fiduciary responsibility as a trustee of diocesan resources, and, much more, he failed to regard himself as a steward of the overall moral and spiritual integrity of the diocese. This overall integrity became disastrously compromised when his need to "pastor" led to a need for secrecy, secrecy became collusion and deceit, and deceit was transmuted, alas, into criminal negligence.

As Christian, adult, women and men, we are to be, at the very least, responsive to the breadth and depth of Christ's spirit. When we succeed in this, we possess an integrity and authenticity that predisposes us to care for the institutions and people we serve in a particular way. This way enables the support and sustenance of the higher nature that is in us and in all people. As professionals we cleave to certain moral principles—truth-telling, promise-keeping, confidence-keeping, and the like—that enable us to apply those personal skills unique to our professional training and experience. We have to be willing to keep ourselves vigilant and diligent in caring about ourselves as professionals and in protecting and promoting the institutions we lead and serve. No small part of this commitment is a willingness and an ability to discern what is being presented to us and what is not. Then we must respond appropriately. An ideologized perspective that, for example, inclines us to read all situations from the convenient and perhaps altogether too innocent role of pastor only can cause us to misstep and possibly do much harm to ourselves and to others. Jesus himself was more than a pastor, and we ourselves are called to be more than pastors. We are called to be fully human, after his fashion, which is more difficult but also more exciting.

I wish to underscore this last point before turning to a more detailed examination of the different counseling contexts in which clergy find themselves. When Ernest Hemingway exhorted those in his own field to take with utmost seriousness their professional responsibilities, he said, "A writer should be of as great probity and honesty as a priest of God."[10] To be held up as priests in such a way is to be reminded again of the greatness and the nobility of our profession. It is also to recognize that our particular profession requires more than we ourselves can ever fully attain, and yet it is right that we keep trying.

The Several Accountabilities of Clergy

Clergy in most denominations find themselves answerable to diverse duties. They are citizens under the laws of their own society; they also have responsibilities to individual members of their families and to their neighbors. As people of broad moral outlook, many clergy feel an accountability to the wider human community. They are accountable to their denominational leadership and denominational policy. They also have an answerability to God as they understand God. Within their congregations, clergy must assume the difficult and sometimes contradictory roles of administrator, preacher, counselor, teacher, worship leader, officiant at specialized ritual functions, friend, and professional colleague, among others.

Even from his or her first day as a professional, a cleric can be in a position of difficulty; a clergy person is not helped by the likelihood that he or she is often sprung upon the Church and world straight from seminary and without benefit of significant apprenticeship. Much of what clergy learn about the practice of their profession is learned on the job; but much of the job itself is implicitly individual or solitary, rather than corporate. For example, I was asked some years ago by the dean of a seminary to allow a seminarian to shadow me on the job for five consecutive days. I declined that proposal on the grounds that since so much of what I do is solitary, I doubted that the seminarian would learn much. I feared also that the student would impose a significant limitation upon the quality of my ministry with people, much like the quality of a psychotherapist's time with people would be limited if an unknown third party were sitting in on a therapy session. (I am uncertain that the ways I spend my time are appropriate for anyone else. The ordained ministry is singular for individuals and circumstances alike.) Moreover, much of what one does when one is "doing" the ministry entails studying, thinking, reading, visiting, and counseling people. These things, though not all that one does, are inherently solitary or at least confidential. Since they are essentially private sorts of things, they call upon a person to respond appropriately as an individual in the unique situation. Whereas we can discuss *some* of these situations with others, no other can join us within them. There is, in other words, a formidable limitation upon what we can learn from and teach to others, owing precisely to the fact that the ordained ministry is so implicitly individual and in many ways confidential.

I may take all kinds of advanced courses in pastoral theology while in seminary. But even so, when I am ordained and find myself standing by the bedside of a dying person, it is specifically I who embody the Christian ministry within a particular historical moment and within a given set of unique personal and family

9

circumstances. With or without previous role plays or clinical pastoral education hints, it is after all *I* who here and now face this person, face the truth that this person uniquely faces. And in faithfulness to the person, to myself, and to the gospel, I do the ministry now needing to be done. It is not chiefly a matter of applying the right pastoral "technology," as perhaps a judge might apply the right law; it is not a matter either of making the right diagnosis or writing the right prescription, as a physician might. The ministry is not so much a matter of making the right applications, though to some degree we acknowledge that there must be an array of appropriate things to do in certain classes of situations. Rather the ministry, as one "does" it, is more about being a certain sort of person in a way that is fitting to one's own sense of self and circumstances. There is, for all that, change and growth as one discovers who one is in the course of carrying out the ministry. Yet even this process of ongoing self-discovery while carrying out one's ministry seems to be largely a solitary business.

We are helped somewhat in our various occasions of ministry by the availability to us of the different *roles* ministers are usually expected to assume. It seems obvious that whenever clergy converse with anyone, one or two of several different roles will be dominant in determining what a minister says and does in response to a given problem. The clergy person assuredly does not assume the same stance in every situation; rather the clergy person *chooses* a particular stance, based upon his or her reading of that given situation. He or she interprets the situation in order to respond appropriately to the need or concern, and upon this interpretation the clergy person plays through the situation as it then begins to unfold.

Sometimes the pastor "reframes" a situation based upon his or her interpretation of what is actually needed. A distraught parishioner, for instance, may ask a pastor why God causes suffering. The pastor may appropriately decide against assuming the teacher role implied by the question taken at face value and instead assume the counselor role in order to respond more effectively to what seems an obvious emotional problem requiring counseling.

To be conscientious, a minister must be continuously alert to the various exigencies and responsibilities that are unique to a situation. The moral and legal obligations falling upon clergy are such that, while we expect clergy to be generally supportive to people in need, we do not expect that they will violate the civil law, violate their conscience, default in their larger responsibilities to the church they serve, and so forth. Nor do we expect others to encourage clergy to do such things. Clergy, we would like to assume, should be reasonably clear-minded about such things as justice, fairness, and personal integrity, simply as members with everyone else of human families, society, and the Church itself.

It is understandably left to the clergy alone to make judgments about what is an appropriate role to play in each situation. Clergy must make judgments as human beings, as professionals, as Christians, as people of conscience before the face of God; we require competence from them in these sorts of matters, and it is right that we do so.

The Different Kinds of Pastoring

When clergy are initially presented with a pastoral problem, the emerging situation must be characterized appropriately so that a fitting response can be made. One set of questions has to do with whether what is needed is pastoral care (that is, mainly support and encouragement) or pastoral counseling (that is, assistance in resolving relationship problems—either with self, others, or God).[11] Indeed, a level of professional psychotherapy beyond the competence of the clergy person may be required. The way a clergy person "reads" the initial situation will govern his or her response. In some cases he or she will sympathize; in other instances the pastor will probe; in still others the pastor will refer to another community resource better suited to respond to the problem presented. In some instances a decision might even be made to combine a pastoral counseling response with the role of administrator of the sacraments, as when somebody is counseled in a matter of guilt and then ritually absolved.

Among the tools for reading the situation is the pastor's instinct concerning the basic nature of the problem being presented and instinct concerning the sort of person making the presentation. Still another factor is the pastor's sense of the scope and limits of his or her expertise. Here the clergy person is helped in knowing that he or she is not generally regarded as a professional within the field of counseling, as would be, for example, a licensed psychologist or a licensed marriage, family, and child counselor. Clergy and professionals within the Church's ministry do perform counseling functions. But from within the counseling field they are regarded as lacking a large amount of training, supervision, expertise, and even time to deal with the deeper emotional problems of people.

Eugene Kennedy identifies clergy as only "paraprofessionals" in counseling since, as professionals in ministry, they encounter people with psychological or emotional problems but have not the same level of competence as psychologists to deal effectively with them.[12] Dr. Harry Bone makes a similar point as he locates the clerical counseling field, in general, between nonmedical psychotherpay (which, he says, responds to "personality problems" without a physical component) and education (which deals with the schooling needs of the "immature or uninstructed").[13] Bone remarks that counseling "is less a profession than a technique or art" used as one facet of the larger responsibilities of those in other professions, including the clergy. The clergy who counsel are treating problems more emotionally complex than can be handled by educational means yet less complex than would warrant treatment by a clinical psychologist.

Assuming that the pastor accepts a role as a pastoral counselor with the parishioner, there is then another set of questions concerned with the issue of how pastoral counseling is distinct from counseling in general. There is enormous confusion surrounding this question even within the churches, and it seems important to clarify it—both in order that the pastor may be more conscious (therefore, one supposes, more effective) in what he or she is doing and in order that the Church as a whole (and its various counselees) may know for themselves more accurately what is going on in the pastoral counseling context.

Unfortunately, there seems to be no clear consensus concerning what makes for *pastoral* counseling. However, theologian John Cobb is particularly lucid in sorting out some essential issues.[14] He begins by describing the mutual suspicions between the disciplines of theology and pastoral counseling. The former, he notes, frequently fails to acknowledge much that is clearly Christian about the latter, whereas many clergy counselors seem to regard the discipline and insights of theology as irrelevant to the counseling tasks undertaken when dealing with troubled people. Cobb remarks that "unfortunately, both suspicions are too well-founded."

Speaking as a theologian, Cobb sympathizes with the difficulties presented to the pastor who preaches God's word in the pulpit but also has to bear with the anguish of counselees in a different setting. Cobb sees the emphases upon administration, the

Church's servant ministry to the world and especially to its poor, and the strengthening of congregational life in community as warranting the same degree of dedication from the pastor as the counseling function.

Cobb says, as if with the more liturgical churches in mind, "Other theologies see the minister as primarily a priest mediating between the divine and the human through a sacramental ministry, whereas pastoral counseling is not sacramental in any obvious sense."[15] The claim that pastoral counseling is not obviously sacramental compels our attention. Yet upon reflection we can accept that nothing, after all, in church doctrine or law connects pastoral counseling precisely with the sacraments or with sacramental rites, though such counseling might accompany a sacramental rite.

Cobb then articulates a view of counseling that is self-consciously rooted in Christian theology, rather than in the assumptions of secular psychotherapy: No matter what techniques are employed in the practice of pastoral counseling, the root assumptions, and therefore, the approach, intention, tone, and the rest of *pastoral* counseling should be clearly informed by Christian theology. When this is the case, counseling by a pastor more clearly becomes "pastoral counseling."

When all of these assumptions and distinctions are better understood and acknowledged, then the Church, the clergy, and counselees will be more clear about what is going on in any given counseling situation. The need to distinguish between what is sacramental and what is not also becomes evident if the Church is to keep its theology straight and if the Church or its clergy should be required to give explanations to a court of civil law. The legal implications of a sacramental act may be quite different from the implications of pastoral counseling; these, in turn, may be different from the implications of providing only pastoral care.

2

The Confession: Its Characteristics and Development through the Church of England

The understanding of what characterizes a confessional situation —what its basic and necessary elements must be, how it is appropriately enacted, what purpose or purposes it is intended to fulfill, and the like—is a matter of continuing discussion not only among various religious denominations but within them. Indeed, careful historical studies by Philippe Delhaye, Cyrille Vogel, and others, show quite clearly that there have been frequent shifts in the meaning of penance throughout the Church's history. These have occurred as pastoral responses have changed to meet new circumstances.[1] The theology of penance has been modified to keep pace with shifting pastoral practices. Such a phenomenon is evident today. In a 1986 news report, for example, the Reverend Dr. Shirley C. Guthrie, professor of systematic theology, Columbia Theological Seminary in Decatur, Georgia, described an emerging change in the understanding of confessional situations. Guthrie characterized this change as a shift in emphasis from one's actions to one's attitudes: "It is not so much the bad things I have done, but it goes beyond that to a confession of wrong attitudes, wrong relationships with my fellow men and God. It is more a question of character than actions."[2]

Not only is this change apparent to the Protestant theologian Guthrie; it is acknowledged by the Roman Catholic priest, the Reverend John Reedy. As the author of a primer for the new rite of penance in the Roman Catholic Church, Reedy presumably broadens, and to some degree relocates, the thrust of sin-as-wrong-act to sin-as-wrong-relationship. (He means wrong relationship with self, others, and God.)[3] An adult of the late twentieth century might find these changes reasonable, even congenial. And yet, considering the tension between the older and the emerging views of confession, it would be helpful to know what is *currently* the ongoing essence of "confession." The historical context within which this matter is taken up has been set by such Anglican writers as Francis G. Belton, Kenneth Ross, and, lately, Martin L. Smith. The Roman Catholic writers Bernard Poschmann, Tad Guzie, John McIlhon, and Robert J. Kennedy should be consulted as well for an overall frame of reference on penance within which confidentiality can be considered.[4]

In the longer view of Christian history, confession has implied a notion of sin. Sin, in turn, has implied a recognition of God's moral claims upon us to do the things belonging to right conduct and good character. Both right conduct and good character entail our being aligned with what has been called "God's will." God's will is thus the primary reference point for determining sin, and sin is the primary problem for which confession poses a possible solution. That people would confess a wrong relationship with others, rather than, say, obtain counseling to rectify an unsatisfactory relationship, would in the Christian understanding imply that right relationships are not only personally significant but that they are also consistent with God's will.

Sin is a broad term, and during the Christian era various emphases have been used to construe its meaning. The concern in some circles today with "right relationship" as an aspect of sin is but one instance of variable historical emphases. Today the dominant Western Christian traditions agree that, whatever the nature of the sin, the following elements constitute a valid religious confession: (1) that the penitent must be sincere in lamenting his or her sins; (2) that there be a sincere intention to amend his or her life so as to avoid further sins if possible; (3) that there be forgiveness or absolution; and (4) that there be confidentiality unless it is properly waived.

Contrition

Each of these elements should be considered more extensively. The first, sincerity in sorrow for sins, implies that a communicant is grieved over a matter that somehow offends against God, other people, or self, all understood as a serious violation of God's will. A violation of some sacred import has occurred in which one's moral standing before God is in question; sincere sorrow is felt, and an admission of guilt is made. The term symbolizing this state of awareness on the part of a penitent is *contrition*. For an admission of this type to be counted as a confession, a number of factors need to be present. One of these is that the confession should be full; that is, the penitent does not deliberately withhold relevant parts of the truth concerning the matter at hand. To do so

16

instead would not only undercut the overall healing effect of the complete confession and the eventual absolution, but also it might simply be misleading and therefore possibly manipulative of the confessor.

In addition to full disclosure, sincerity also implies the penitent's lively sense of the justice of God, God's holiness and righteousness, even God's honor. The basic Christian understanding of sorrow for sin, derived from the Bible and church history, includes a feeling for the seriousness of violating human or church community (which is also God's community) and so for violating one's own relationship with God.

One way the Roman Catholic moral theologians have analyzed this as a confessional issue is through contrition and attrition. The *Encyclopedia of Religion*[5]—one of many Roman Catholic documents addressing this issue—defines attrition as, "in medieval theology, that sorrow for sin, which, in distinction from contrition, is incomplete or motivated by fear of penalty rather than by love of God."[6] Attrition might, for instance, be characterized as the sincere sorrow and grief of someone discovered in the act of committing a crime who, because of the foreseeable punitive consequences of being discovered, now wishes he or she had not committed the crime in the first place. In this example, the regret, though sincere, is a response to the fear of punishment rather than a moral or spiritual response of grief concerning the violation itself. Still, for Roman Catholics, sincere grief and regret even of a self-serving nature—which is attrition— is a sufficient reason to make a confession. Such a confession must, however, be followed by penance. What, then, is to protect against the reduction of the confession to the level of gesture alone? How might we recognize, value, and commend the true healing potential of a person's being genuinely sorry for the sins themselves?

The Roman Catholic theologian Karl Rahner explains that within the Roman Catholic community, attrition by itself is not a sufficient basis for the valid reception of the sacrament of penance.[7] Rather, the Roman sacrament of penance itself helps us to feel genuine sorrow for our sins. This may be best understood in light of the scholastic notion of *ex attrito fit contritus, vi clavium*—one's initial attrition subsequently becomes a genuine contrition over the sin itself, owing to the transformative power of the sacrament. The Roman Catholic theologian Avery Dulles puts it this way: "The sacrament produces the contrition it expresses, and only by doing so can it become a genuine expression both of man's repentance and God's powerful mercy toward man."[8]

The Protestants, possessing a less thoroughgoing view of the Church and its sacraments, resisted the attrition-contrition distinction. For the Protestants, either we are sincere or we are not. Therefore, the Catholic *Encyclopedia of Religion* rightly notes that the doctrine of attrition was rejected outright by Protestant theologians.[9] A person's simple sincerity is the emphasis through which Protestant moral theology proceeds, and thus, we may stipulate as a Protestant view that an essential component in the confessional context is simply contrition, a sincere regret concerning one's sin or sins *per se,* a genuine sense of violation of one's life before God and/or of one's relatedness to others as fellow members of God's beloved Creation.

The Anglican development of contrition begins with Richard Hooker (1554–1600), "the first great theologian of Anglican tradition," who "interpreted the *Book of Common Prayer* to future generations and thus contributed to the formation of Anglican spirituality."[10] Book 6 of Hooker's *Of the Laws of Ecclesiastical Polity* contains his essential thinking on the subject of contrition. He had announced earlier that our membership in the Church places us where we can participate in the life of God, through Christ, by the Holy Spirit—which is the way we fulfill our life's chief aim. As part of the Church, we are, in fact, participants in the redeemed humanity of Christ, the Second Adam. The Holy Spirit continually creates and recreates the Church as the Body of Christ. The Spirit's operations upon us, as church members, helps to keep all of us in the realm of salvation and away from sin. This basic understanding is the context within which Hooker considers contrition, repentance, or, as he sometimes calls it, penitence.

For Hooker, contrition is "the aversion of the will from sin." The crucial element within us that disposes us appropriately toward God is "the inward secret repentance of the heart."[11] Our contrition is evoked by God's grace. Our response of contrition is the consequence of both fear and love toward God, with love ultimately becoming predominant. Here we can see a decided shift away from the Roman view of the Sacrament of Penance toward a more Protestant understanding of the direct operations of God's grace upon us, within the overall church context. In an oft-quoted passage, Hooker writes this:

18

From these considerations, setting before our eyes our inexcusable both unthankfulness in disobeying so merciful, and foolishness in provoking so powerful a God, there ariseth necessarily a pensive and corrosive desire that we had done otherwise; a desire which suffereth us to foreslow no time, to feel no quietness within ourselves, to take neither sleep nor food with contentment, never to give over supplications, confessions, and other penitent duties, till the light of God's reconciled favour shine in our darkened soul (VI.3.4).[12]

The entire process of repentance, having begun with a deep and sincere sense of averting one's will from sin (i.e., contrition), then continues with our confession ("submission of ourselves to God by supplication and prayer") and concludes with satisfaction ("the purpose of a new life, testified with present works of amendment").[13]

The possibility of a private, auricular confession, in Hooker's thinking, is made available specifically to those who are susceptible to the sin of *scrupulosity* (a sinful obsession with sinfulness). That is, God has mercifully "consecrated persons, which by sentence of power and authority given from above, may as it were out of his very mouth ascertain timorous and doubtful minds in their own particular, cure them of all their scrupulosities, leave them settled in peace and satisfied touching the mercy of God towards them" (VI.6.1.7).[14] Here, what is for Rome the Sacrament of Penance becomes instead a concession to human weakness in scrupulosity. Embracing the Anglican view that there are only two sacraments, Hooker regards the evocative love of God as arousing our contrition as we participate chiefly in that great sacramental act of corporate worship, the eucharist.

In analyzing the overall departure from the Roman view and the development of contrition, beginning with Hooker and continuing through John Donne and George Herbert (1593–1633), John Booty concludes that for Anglicans "contrition is more than an isolated act of piety." As opposed to the Roman emphasis of the unitary act of contrition within the Sacrament of Penance, this Anglican view regards contrition as "fundamental to that worship of God which is a life long *latria,* service towards God, our neighbors, and the rest of creation."[15] Contrition is an "on-going sense we have of our openness to God, of gratitude for what God has done and continues to do; it is a continuing servant ministry of praise, responsive to God and to the needs of the world." Contrition is appropriately nurtured as a continuing aspect of our "lively faith": We are liberated and empowered

19

in Christian service, and we engage in corporate worship, constantly saying the general confession as contrite persons within the Church.

In the Episcopal Church's Teaching Series volume entitled *Liturgy for Living,* professors Charles Price and Louis Weil announce the "utmost importance" of the "quality of relations" between Christian women and men.[16] They ground this quality upon the interiority of Christian life—upon our being truly "in love and charity" with our neighbors. Because of the deeply individual and personal nature of Christian life thus understood, one's sin is to be seen as an intensely serious "mark of alienation, not only from God but also from neighbors."[17] Therefore, it is crucial for the Church to offer God's forgiveness ceaselessly. What helps to keep things honest and healthful for both the Episcopal Church pastor and the communicant in the confessional context is the contrition of the penitent—the penitent's genuine sorrow for the sin itself.

Repentance

A sincere intention to amend one's life to avoid sin if possible is the essential meaning of penitence or repentance, as these terms are usually employed in religious discourse. St. Ambrose defined penitence as *"mourning of man for the sin that he has done, and the resolve to do no more anything for which he ought to mourn."* The key to penitence, or repentance, is personal responsibility both for acceptance of one's agency in having committed a sin and for resolve in amending one's life.

The Roman Catholic canons of the Council of Trent contain a precise distinction between one's guilt before God (*culpa*), which under the right conditions could be removed by absolution, and one's prospect of temporal punishment (*poena*) owing to the consequences of sinful actions. Indeed, the Latin authorities thought that God's eternal justice might well dictate that we should submit willingly to earthly punishment for our sins. Sincere repentance, understood as both contrition and the genuine intention to amend life, is necessary if one is to become reconciled to God. Being thus reconciled, however, according to Trent, guarantees no escape by the sinner from the requirements of temporal justice.

We might be instructed at this juncture by recent public "confessions" on the part of both high level "Contragate" politicians and media evangelists. Some, speaking with irony, hold that when these persons "confess" to being responsible for something they are actually issuing "no-fault confessions."[18] "Confessions" of this sort convey insincere proclamations of responsibility for some act and a presumed sense of regret, but their primary purpose is to close discussion upon whatever self-serving endeavors are now coming under public scrutiny. A Christian analysis of the "no-fault confession" is that it is non-contrition, a gesture only. A valid confession *must* entail a sincere commitment to cease committing sinful acts or cultivating harmful attitudes, as one instead sets forth to amend one's life.

Absolution

Still another element essential to a valid confessional situation is the act of absolution or forgiveness, announced by some person or persons authorized to do so or perhaps pronounced by the injured party. To absolve someone is to recognize the power of sin to violate one's relationship with God and to violate human community, together with the need for the restoration of that which was violated. A confession, therefore, includes the deep desire to be restored to right relationship with God and human community and to be set free for a new future in one's own life with God, the wider community, and one's self.

The Protestant emphasis regarding absolution, following Luther and Calvin, has been on the declaration of God's forgiveness as a gift of grace already accomplished by Christ. Roman Catholic theology, however, has emphasized a priest's "giving" absolution as an act of the Church. The priest's absolution thus signifies one's reconciliation with God because, in Roman Catholic theology, one is now reconciled with the Church. The absolution is pronounced in the indicative mood these days in the Western Catholic church. Catholic theologians are careful, however, to differentiate between God's forgiveness and a priest's absolution; absolution is "the action of the church congruent with the action of God."[19] Anglicans have decidedly placed themselves within the Protestant tradition, retaining the Roman term *absolution* in certain liturgical rituals but embracing the Protestant theological notion of God's once-and-for-all-time forgiveness. (See the specifics on the Anglican development in the section "The Confession in Anglicanism," below).

Confidentiality

A final element in a valid confession is the assurance of confi-

21

dentiality, unless, in certain circumstances, confidentiality is properly waived. It goes without saying that as the deeply human, sincere, and honest disclosures of our hearts, secrets must be protected from public review, but the rationales that support what we know intuitively about keeping confidences are relatively few in number.

In ethics, the importance of keeping confidences has been argued from the "rule" basis that promise-keeping and autonomy-honoring are intrinsically right. Alternatively, the case has been argued on the consequentialist ground that a good way to maintain the integrity and reputation of self and profession, or a good way to make more effective the Church's ministry, is to retain confidences. That a general duty exists to keep confidences cannot be doubted. The magnitude of that duty can be a matter of some disagreement when competing duties arise in different circumstances. For example, the ethicist LeRoy Walters notes that "in both law and ethics the duty to preserve confidentiality is generally considered to be only a prima facie duty—one that can be overridden by other, more compelling duties in certain circumstances."[20] Walters indicates the three most commonly used grounds for violating a confidence: to protect the client; to protect another (third party); to protect society at large. He adds that these grounds are "more compelling when they are forward looking . . . than backward looking."[21] Indeed, today in the United States, the public's much-discussed (and presumed) right to know is in large measure a protest against the possible harmful consequences of allowing confidential information to remain out of sight. This protest has apparently been persuasive, for it has resulted in the Freedom of Information Act passed in the United States in 1966 and fortified in 1974.

Surely, a sincere respect for people, their autonomy and their privacy, and a lively apprehension regarding the hurt that may befall another when we are indiscreet will cause us to respect confidences, especially confidences made within pastoral counseling, and most especially in confessional contexts. When confidences are to be breached, the confiding party must give free consent. In a situation where all elements of a valid confession are present and there is no valid waiver, it seems virtually impossible to justify a unilateral breach of confidentiality.

The Confession in Anglicanism

Of particular interest is the way the confessional situation is

22

understood within the Anglican tradition and the Episcopal Church in the United States. We can gain insight into this by analyzing the historical struggle between those who, in the Reformation tradition, advocated the adequacy of a "general confession" primarily and those who fought to preserve private confession to a priest alone.

From at least the eighth century onward, the Western Catholic view has been that reconciliation with the Church (through absolution by its priests) was congruent with the very forgiveness of God; therefore, confession to a priest was a matter of the soul's eternal salvation or damnation. It is no wonder that, with eternity put seriously into question, some of the faithful began to exhibit scrupulosity. As is well known, by the Reformation period, many bishops and priests were accepting money from penitents in ways not always morally commendable. Martin Luther, precisely because of the corruption attendant upon private confessions to priests, set about to reform the Church. He announced his great relief at rescuing Christian people from "the great eternal torture" of the obligation to confess to priests and the overall "terrible domination of the clergy over the laity."[22]

As Episcopal Church theologians Charles Price and Louis Weil have it, "the English reformers, like their Lutheran and Calvinist counterparts, dismantled [this] system."[23] Accepting that forgiveness of sins was accomplished by God once and for all in Christ, the English Reformers established general confessions in public worship. Absolution was complete and without limit as people were encouraged to acknowledge their various sins privately during the time of general confession in public worship.

Marion Hatchett brings out, in his 1979 *Commentary on the American Prayer Book,* that the 1548 Order of the Communion, the 1549 Prayer Book, and the 1552 revision all contain the general confession and absolution.[24] Beginning with the 1548 order, private confessions were no longer mandatory. The 1549 book and all the books following did provide for private confession in the case of a sick person visited by a priest. The rubric regarding private confession and absolution for the sick was dropped from the first American book. It reappeared subsequently in the "Office for the Visitation of the Sick" in the 1928 book. The development, first in the English and then in the American church, was clearly away from private confessions.

John T. McNeill's magisterial *History of the Cure of Souls* develops in meticulous detail "the cure of souls in the Anglican communion."[25] In outline, his relevant analysis is this: The requirement of penance (understood as private confession to a Roman Catholic priest) was enjoined by the 1536 *Articles About Religion.* A year later, *The Institution of a Christian Man* proclaimed that penance was not always necessary. By 1543 *A Necessary Doctrine and Erudition for any Christian Man,* known as "The King's Book," picked up the Reformers' emphasis on the affairs regarding penance as purely a matter of one's inward state. This book established the Anglican position firmly on that understanding, thereby aligning the English church with the continental Reformers on this issue.[26]

Private confession, according to McNeill, was considered discretionary in the 1552 Prayer Book, being viewed by this time as "exceptional rather than regular." McNeill finds no clear indication of the place of private auricular confession in sixteenth-century England, nor of any strong push to abolish it. With J.R.H. Moorman,[27] McNeill does take up the confession and confidentiality connection, as it is given in Canon 113 of the Canons of 1604 (sometimes called the Canons of 1603, and sometimes called the 1604 Series). In its original context, this canon addressed the regular obligation of local clergy to report parishioner-offenders to *church* superiors ("The Ordinary") for discipline. This is the original place in the history of Church of England canon law in which confidentiality is made a duty for English clergy. According to both McNeil and Moorman, the purpose of Canon 113 is then to relieve the parish priest (otherwise obliged to report bad behavior to the bishop) of this duty internal to the discipline of the church. The means to this end is obtained by the confession of the offender, which the priest is then bound to keep secret—secret, that is, from the bishop. There is no reference in Canon 113 to privileged communication in what is known in the United States as a court of civil law, and no mention is made of any canon law binding secrecy by clergy from an official of the civil court. The one exception to the binding of a priest within a church context is when the priest's own life would otherwise be placed in danger: Then he may break the "seal."

It is important to note that these English canons are sometimes cited to support the presumed inviolability within all Anglicanism of the "seal of confession." Further, the canons are regarded by some as inhibiting the compulsion of testimony in a civil court of law. Overlooked or ignored is that these canons referred

24

explicitly to a matter of internal church discipline. Even as such, there appears to be a serious moral question involved here because of a possible coercion to confess—a coercion proceeding from the threat otherwise of church discipline. That is, under the circumstances described in these canons, questions of free consent and therefore also of full contrition are raised. Common sense may easily suppose that coercion undermines both. Noteworthy, too, is the fact that according to these canons the "seal" is not altogether binding in every case but rather admits of a unilateral exception (regarding the priest's life). The exception to the seal (even within the church discipline context alone) was taken by Roman Catholic experts as evidence that the Church of England was weakening the absolute force of the "seal" and that it was doing so because the civil courts, beginning in the seventeenth century were compelling testimony in any case.[28]

Though the 1969 canons for the Church of England contain a "Proviso to Canon 113" for today's English church, there is also on the record this remark of a high official of the Church of England, the Archbishop of Canterbury, Geoffrey Fisher, issued in 1959: "Priests have no statutory right to refuse to answer a judge in a court of law." Mindful of the tendency to advert to the seventeenth-century warrant for secrecy, the archbishop continues, "The present canon governing secrecy of the confessional dates from 1603 and is regarded as largely obsolete."[29]

The English Reformers

The various nuances of confession and confidentiality through English history are instructive. Thomas Cranmer (d. 1556) did not regard private confession to a priest as an obligation based on scriptural authority but said it must be done if one desired priestly absolution. John Jewel (d. 1571) was quite opposed to private confessions, regarding them as a "rack of men's consciences to the maintenance of their tyranny."[30] Richard Hooker (d. 1600) allowed for private confession to a priest in the case of the visitation of the sick or in cases where the sin of scrupulosity required it; Hooker saw the priest's role in the matter of absolution to be that of assurance of "God's most gracious and merciful pardon."[31] McNeill summarizes the views of the English Reformation leaders this way: "Most of what Anglicans wrote about confession was highly tinged by anti-Roman polemic."[32]

At this juncture it might be helpful to introduce the careful analysis of the esteemed Episcopal Church historian John E. Booty

25

and his documentation of what he calls the English Reformers' rejection of sacramental confession.[33] Booty chronicles the successful Anglican attack upon "sacramental confession," claiming this to be but the first victory of a "moral revolution, a radical change affecting the future development of Anglican moral theology."[34] Booty contends that though some of the English Reformers were too extravagant in their condemnation of this "legalistic, Pelagian, laxist, and magical" institution, their dominant criticism of sacramental confession was simply of "its fundamental nature." Sacramental penance "was designed to console the sinner and it did not."[35] The Reformers embraced instead what they called "the true, lively, and Christian Faith," which is to say, the gospel.

The differentiation between the Roman Sacrament of Penance as an instance of dead faith and the lively faith of the Christian gospel may have appeared first in Thomas Cranmer's *First Book of Homilies* (1547), from which Booty quotes extensively. Booty himself comments,

> The lively faith has no need of sacramental confession and, indeed, stands in danger of being corrupted if not destroyed by the legalistical Pelagianism of the Sacrament of Penance. Correct moral behavior is not bred of the imposition of moral and legal norms, but rather of faith in God.[36]

Both Cranmer and Richard Hooker decisively worked out the liturgical forms and theological foundations for Anglicanism: What before had passed only between priest and penitent alone in the confessional became an aspect of corporate worship before the face of God. The peculiarly Anglican treatment of the matter was that contrition was evoked in corporate worship through the encounter with God's Word and sacraments (i.e., baptism and eucharist). Being made contrite as individuals in community with other worshiping Christians, we ask together for forgiveness. Booty continues, "What the contrite and penitent faithful ought to do in specific cases as a result of this penitence is not dictated in any detail. For most it is enough that they persist in communion with God. . . ."[37] For the Reformers in general,

> no priest gives specific instructions, no penance is meted out, no satisfaction is presented, although quite clearly what shall be done under the guidance of God's Spirit shall witness to God's glory and be in obedience to the holy law directing us to love God and neighbor.[38]

The Roman church had placed great emphasis upon the "power of the keys," which refers to Jesus' conferring upon some (subsequently the priest alone) the power to bind and to loose people and their sins in the private confession. The Reformers challenged such a notion. With Hugh Latimer and John Jewel, the "keys" were no longer a matter of the priest's prerogative in the confessional; rather, in Anglicanism, all that was implied by the "keys" became the preacher's prerogative in preaching—preaching, that is, the gospel of God's forgiveness.[39] The openness, the community-based, corporate context within which affairs of sin and forgiveness were treated became a chief characteristic marking Anglicanism as a distinct way within the larger body of Christian denominations in the world. Provision was made for private confessions in Anglicanism where these seemed appropriate. But the main thrust of thought and practice regarding confession and the announcement of forgiveness, of contrition and absolution and all the other things implied by the problem of sinfulness, was to locate these matters squarely within the context of corporate worship.

The changes now accomplished regarding the former Sacrament of Penance were made decisively by the English Reformers in such a way as to mark the Anglican Church uniquely. Anglicans were chiefly to live their lives based on a lively faith in God, who nurtures and liberates, rather than on the private confession to a priest and the slavishness either to priest or to the scrupulosity that might imply. Booty concludes, "As it matured Anglicanism affirmed . . . the insistence on the necessity of human freedom alongside the necessity of grace to enable humanity in the exercise of that freedom in turning from evil, in choosing the Good." In service to this crucial project, "sacramental confession as preached at the end of the Middle Ages was rejected and emphasis placed upon the Christian, living in the community of the faithful, assisted by Word and sacraments, making moral judgments, personal and social. This was the lively faith to which Cranmer referred. . . ."[40]

The Post-Reformation Period

The seventeenth-century Anglican writers continued in an identical vein.[41] When Archbishop William Laud (d. 1645) proposed a rule for the Scottish church that approximated the Canons of 1604, he was accused of promoting a "popish confession." Jeremy Taylor (d. 1667) believed that private confession to a priest could be very beneficial to some in certain instances; he was so respectful of the "seal" that he counseled that a confessant should refrain from confessing any actions whose descriptions to a priest might qualify as an exception to the seal. In *Unum Necessarium or Doctrine of Repentance* (1655), Taylor advised that priests should not be placed in the position of divulging confidences owing to their having heard things excepted from the seal's protection. He continued that priests, furthermore, should not have to be otherwise unfairly oppressed with burdensome information. In any case, in his *Dissuasive from Popery* (1664–67) Taylor rejected the Roman Catholic view that full confession was everyone's proper duty.

Archbishop H. R. McAdoo, Anglican primate of Ireland, has considered the seventeenth-century Anglican moral theogians' treatment of repentance. He describes their attempt to continue the tradition of Cranmer, Hooker, and others, as they rediscovered and applied the New Testament understanding of repentance: The seventeenth-century Anglicans "took the emphasis off sacramental penance and placed it firmly on repentance as a virtue and as a major element in the new life of obedience in love."[42] This was a continuation and reinforcement of the "lively faith" accent as developed by Cranmer and Hooker. McAdoo acknowledges a "range of emphasis" in the way this matter is worked out in the seventeenth-century but asserts that "the positive line is unmistakable." These theologians "saw repentance and faith as being so close as to be interdependent."[43] Martin Thornton's analysis is that the Caroline theologians' chief objection to the Roman Catholic position on repentance was that Catholics had replaced theology with law. In contrast, Anglican Caroline thought "was interested not so much in rigorous moral life as in the glory of God whose service is perfect freedom."[44]

McAdoo identifies three features distinctive to Caroline casuistry: the primacy of individual conscience and personal responsibility; the importance of reason in determining moral responsibility; and a tendency to "reasonable tutiorism." (*Tutiorism* is an inclination, when faced with competing alternatives, to choose the "safer way" [*opinio tutior*]. This means assuming that the *apparently* relevant moral principle applies to the case at hand, rather than that it does not, unless after diligent analysis the contrary determination then seems obvious.) Going further in characterizing seventeenth-century Anglican casuistry, McAdoo writes, "Also noteworthy is the *explicit insistence* that casuistry must be based on Scripture and reason and not upon 'authorities' and canon law."[45] This "insistence" was part of the overall Anglican move away from the Roman emphasis and toward a "Practical Divinity," as they called it. By this term they meant to ground moral and spiritual life in the worshiping community. Devotion in common worship and practical direction were intertwined. How Anglicans disposed themselves in practical affairs was a correlate of their personal piety, their lively faith, as sustained within the context of corporate worship. Common prayer, individual prayer (in recognition, nonetheless, of one's being part of a worshiping community), meditation, scripture reading, confession, acceptance of God's forgiving grace, amendment of life, service to others, and the rest were all parts of one corporate worship fabric. In this, the seventeenth century Anglicans sustained and strengthened the peculiarly Anglican development begun by the earlier English Reformers.

McNeill finds that "Anglican testimony on the cure of souls in the eighteenth century is almost as abundant as in the seventeenth. There is in it very little of material importance that is at all new."[46] Gerald R. Cragg, in his book *The Church and the Age of Reason, 1648–1789,* describes the early eighteenth century as one in which the Church indulged the rationalist tendencies of the surrounding culture.[47] The interesting developments in English church history at this time were the emerging intellectual currents in theology and a growing skepticism concerning clergy appointments and prerogatives. The later eighteenth century was not particularly noteworthy with respect to our present concern, or perhaps any other concern either: "The second half of the century saw a pronounced decline in the vigour and distinction in English religious thought. There are few important movements and few great names."[48] Altogether, according to Cragg, "the eighteenth-century was a relatively static age. . . ."[49]

The nineteenth-century evangelical revival in England continued the momentum to devalue private confession. The Oxford movement, however, led by Edward Bouverie Pusey, sought to restore the Roman Catholic notion of penance as a sacrament and the Roman practice of private confession. To promote these ideas, Pusey in 1877 published his own adaptation of a Roman Catholic book, Abbe Jean Joseph Gaume's *Manual for Confessors* (1854), and attempted to transport the Roman Catholic theological apparatus and practice concerning the "Sacrament of Penance" into the Anglican tradition.

There was much resistance to the Oxford movement's interest in introducing Roman Catholic practices into the Church of England, including the "Sacrament of Penance." Anti-Roman sentiment was widespread in England. The zeal of those who resisted and sometimes persecuted the ritualists, as the Oxford people were called, led to excesses against sincere and devout high church people. This, in turn, evoked a tide of sentiment in favor of tolerance of the "Anglo-Catholic" positions. The feelings of some partisans—the extreme Anglo-Catholics and the extreme evangelicals alike—kept the liturgical (and thus the doctrinal) pot boiling for years in England. Archbishop of Canterbury Randall Davidson in the early twentieth century persuaded Prime Minister Balfour to appoint the Royal Commission on Ecclesiastical Discipline to try to sort things out. This commission ended up recommending that the Church of England conservatives propose changes in liturgy and in the new ecclesiastical courts.

The slowness of church decision making in this area, the advent of the First World War, eventual parliamentary debate (and rejection) of church recommendations, and an overall inability and/or unwillingness of the church leadership to command and so resolve the situation, meant that Pusey's agenda, and that of its detractors, never did receive either vindication or condemnation. Alex Vidler, an eminent historian of the period, remarks of Archbishop Davidson that, "while he was prepared to see the thing through if possible, he regarded it as a clerical preoccupation to which the laity were more or less indifferent, and he sympathized with them. Who will say that he was wrong?"[50] Not I.

McNeill describes the current Anglican position on confession and absolution as "unresolved." He provides a bit more detail. At the request of the bishop of London, a scholarly conference was held from December 29 to January 1, 1901, at Fulham Palace. Most conferees were divided between commending private confession or regarding it as appropriate only in exceptional instances. A third view, advanced by H. Hensley Henson, was that the Church should be worried about priests who genuinely believe that they have the power to absolve sins. There was no clear resolution at Fulham. Clearly, though, in neither the current English Prayer Book nor the Alternate Service Book is there a ceremony providing for the reconciliation of a penitent.

Withal, the basic issues remain the same as they have been since the English Reformation, and they tend to be based essentially upon one's view of the Church. If the Roman Catholic doctrine seems persuasive, the Church truly would have an authority of absolution congruent with God's own forgiveness of sins. In this understanding, one would then have to regard the validity of the priest's unique role as the "giver" of absolution and also would then be pressed to regard private confession to a priest as crucial to the soul's salvation. One would be hard-pressed to imagine any duty to breach confidentiality as more compelling than protecting those things pertaining to eternal salvation.

This Roman Catholic emphasis, however, does not seem to be the foundation upon which the Church of England has operated. The English church has historically regarded the Thirty-nine Articles as indicative of its basic self-understanding. Article 25 of these reads, "There are two sacraments ordained of Christ Our Lord in the Gospel, that is to say baptism and the supper of the Lord. Those five commonly called sacraments, that is to say . . . penance . . . are not to be counted for sacraments of the Gospel." This article, placing penance in a less significant position than it is in the Roman church, plus the great weight of the tradition, as shown above, clearly aligns the church with the Protestant emphasis of the English Reformers. The more "pastoral" argument encouraging people to undertake private confession for their own welfare seems more characteristically Anglican than the ecclesiological argument of Roman theology, which brings together in a more grave fashion personal salvation, private confession, sacraments, priests, church, and the forgiveness of God.

The Protestant emphasis upon sin and forgiveness in the Anglican tradition locates the great weight of the matter upon the atoning sacrifice of Christ. Here only is the effective forgiveness of God for human sins. The Reverend John Stott writes, "Confessing . . . sins to a priest is not right, since it makes a secret confession not secret through including another person and a public confession not public through excluding the church."[51] Stott's more evangelical position within the Anglican church regards private confession to a priest as a confusion concerning one's direct access to Christ, a false glorification of the priest, and a derogation of Jesus Christ, his uniqueness and absolute authority. The sum of it is, in the words of the familiar Anglican formulation regarding private confession, "all may, some should, none must"—which, relative to the absoluteness of the Roman view, seems more a victory for the Protestant emphasis.

3

Confession in the Episcopal Church

The Episcopal Church in the United States has a significant history relating to confession. Because there are those who identify strongly with one or another of the partisan positions of several years ago, I believe I should state my own position before presenting the following material. That way there will be less likelihood that I might seem to be building a case somewhat guilefully for one side or the other.

My view is that any priest validly using the present 1979 prayer book rite, the "Reconciliation of a Penitent," should never divulge to anyone the contents of a private confession. I cannot conceive of any priest allowing any exception, except in the most extraordinary instance. A *subsequent* related conversation initiated by the penitent about, say, what might be done positively to ameliorate the circumstances of injury, grief, or whatnot could, of course, count as a counseling session, by common agreement, apart from the confession and ritual reconciliation itself. From this sort of session, divulgences might proceed by mutual agreement, in accordance with common sense.

I have thought carefully about what extraordinary instance might cause me to violate the seal of confession. I could imagine, for example, living as I do only a few miles from California's gas chamber at San Quentin prison, that if I had received information "under the seal" that someone on death row were innocent, I might very well divulge that information. Admittedly, that exception is based upon an extremely unlikely circumstance, but I have already indicated that any such exception would have to be utterly extreme. My reasons for breaking the seal in an instance like this could have to do with what Jesus had in mind when he subordinated the sabbath law to the exigencies of human necessity. These reasons would also have to do with my belief that no rule, no matter how apparently comprehensive, in fact anticipates every contingency and tragic circumstance of human life. They would have to do, finally, with my sense that I am more faithful and more fully human when I am accountable to the merciful and forgiving Christ than when I am accountable to inflexible and impersonal rules. Certainly there are many valid reasons for obeying rules almost all of the time; but we are still called to a life of responsible freedom, beyond a life of legalism. This commonsense notion was recognized by Jesus himself, most notably when he healed on the sabbath, and it has since been recognized by such diverse others as Martin Luther, Søren Kierkegaard, Martin Luther King, Jr., Dietrich Bonhoeffer, and, though not in theological terms, by the Nuremberg court.

The rules articulated by the Church are compelling precisely because they are based upon the life of Christ, Christ's teachings, and the theologians, who, we say in faith, have labored under the influence of God's Holy Spirit. One does not abrogate those rules lightly but only after the most searching, rigorous, and painstaking care. The fact is, though, that God's revelation is ongoing, and therefore for *theological* reasons, one affirms with James Russell Lowell that "new occasions teach new duties." We are called to worship the living God; we are not called in an ultimate sense to worship rules. We are called to take sincere and serious account of the rules; we are not called to ignore them. We are called to be faithful in the new circumstances to which God has brought us; occasionally, and then only after the most diligent analysis, we *might* transgress a rule.

Having said all this, being as honest as I can about my basic beliefs and approach to life, I must admit this apparent paradox: I *can* imagine that I might break the seal, given some bizarre set of circumstances; I *cannot* imagine, however, practically speaking, that I would ever encounter such circumstances in my lifetime. All this is to say that I assent to the inviolability of the seal of confession completely—but I do not give assent to that rule idolatrously.

The U.S. Prayer Book and the Seal

In our world of human foible and tragedy, pressure may indeed fall upon the confessor to divulge something learned within the context of the prayer book service for the "Reconciliation of a Penitent." The applicable rubric for this rite is as follows: "The content of a confession is not normally a matter of subsequent discussion. The secrecy of a confession is morally absolute for a confessor, and must under no circumstances be broken." (The rubric's reference is apparently to that notion of binding secrecy sometimes identified in church history as "the seal of confession," though that exact term is not used here.) *The Oxford Dictionary of the Christian Church* defines the "seal" precisely as an "absolute obligation" of secrecy concerning "anything said by a penitent using the sacrament of penance."[1] The narrow focus in the *Dictionary* article upon the Roman church's "Sacrament of Penance" is then broadened by the *Oxford Dictionary* to include for the English church the "relevant proviso" to the Church of England's 1603 canons (Canon 113).

It is necessary to analyze the American rubric carefully. First, one must assume that a sincere confession has taken place—that contrition (the sincere sorrow for sin), repentance, and the like, did indeed characterize the confessant's attitude within the confessional situation and that there was no deliberate attempt to deceive or manipulate the confessor. This assumption must be granted because the rubric immediately preceding the injunction to secrecy specifies that the penitent already "has given evidence of due contrition."

The secrecy then enjoined here does not by any means preclude further discussion of the confession. The priest is normally enjoined from initiating the discussion, but he or she may discuss the matter with the penitent later, since, "if the penitent wishes to reopen the subject with the confessor, this may be done" (according to Hatchett's *Commentary on the American Prayer Book,* generally regarded as the authoritative interpretative commentary.)[2]

It is interesting to note further that even in the Roman Catholic Church the seal allows of some exceptions. Thus, according to the Roman Catholic *Encyclopedia of Religion,* the seal of confession is "the most strict obligation of keeping entirely secret everything said by the penitent in confession for the purpose of obtaining absolution."[3] The article then continues, "Without the free consent of the penitent, the priest who heard the penitent's confession may not in any way use this information, not even to save himself from the threat of death." But the "free consent of the penitent" is, of course, a waiver of confidentiality—even of confidentiality under the seal.

Although there are many differences of opinion regarding the seal, the relevant issues have not been rigorously addressed by today's theologians and ethicists in the Episcopal Church. Indeed, to find a comprehensive treatment of the seal one must consult an earlier generation of theologians. Prominent among these is

Francis J. Hall, author of *The Sacraments* and at one time a professor of dogmatic theology at the General Theological Seminary.[4] Professor Hall notes in his work the possibility that a priest might break the seal—at least with respect to a confession's contents, though not with respect to the confessant's identity. Hall writes, "Even when it may be necessary for a priest to consult with another priest in order to deal wisely with his penitent, he is under obligation to avoid betrayal of the penitent's identity."[5] Hall goes on to describe some of the exceptions to the binding nature of the seal: (1) When the priest knows what has been confessed, from personal experience of it outside the confessional then the communication may not be regarded as sealed; (2) "when the good of others can thus be promoted, and the penitent freely consents; the seal may be broken for such good, but not further"; and (3) "when the confession clearly reveals intention to commit in the future a crime that endangers others, it is widely held that such information does not come under the seal."[6] Hall's second point holds the danger of a "slippery slope." The priest's utilitarian presumption of the good of others *could* open the door to unwise abuses. However, especially noteworthy here is that this second point clearly provides for a waiver to break the seal and that the third point mentions a "widely held" view that the priest may unilaterally decide that a piece of information is not, in fact, "sealed"; moreover, in this sort of instance the priest may acknowledge the rights of innocent third parties.

At about the time Professor Hall was writing, a commission on doctrine in the Church of England was generating the report *Doctrine in the Church of England: The Report of the Commission on Christian Doctrine appointed by the Archbishops of Canterbury and York in 1922.*[7] In this document, which offers implicit guidance to Episcopal Church clergy, the broad view of private confession was set forth: "The authoritative teaching of the Church of England neither enjoins nor advises the regular and universal practice of auricular confession."[8] The commission stated this concerning private auricular confession heard by a priest: "The confession is heard under the seal of absolute secrecy. . . . This, however, does not necessarily imply that he [the priest] ought not in certain cases to refuse absolution except on condition of the disclosure by the penitent or with his consent of certain facts; the determination of the cases, if any, in which he should so act is one of the most delicate problems of moral theology, which it would be outside our province to discuss."[9] What seems to be allowed here is the possibility that a priest might coerce a penitent into disclosing "certain facts" or himself disclose certain facts "with his [the penitent's] consent." The threat evidently exists here to withhold absolution and/or to place the confessant outside the favor of the Church, and/or perhaps leave the confessant without whatever confidentiality protections would have been viable if the confessional situation had otherwise proceeded to its completion—to an absolution and binding secrecy.

The point is that, although many might wish it otherwise, exceptions to the presumably airtight seal of confession have been and are provided for. *Who* authorizes exceptions and what potential these exceptions might have for engendering policy are still open questions. The church's institutional identity and integrity would seem to require as much definition as possible. Yet it is in the area of pastoral care (where these issues tend to arise) that canonical legislation so patently and so frequently fails to meet the case.

Rubrics, Ritual, and Law in the U.S. Episcopal Church

At a different level, and with attention to an ecclesiastical matter, the question intrudes, What is the force of a rubric after all? If a rubric is only a ceremonial direction, then the rubric formally, within itself, constitutes only a weak sanction for keeping secrecy. If, on the other hand, a rubric, qua rubric, counts the same as a church law, then formally, within itself, the rubric states a heavy injunction of the Church that could be disregarded by a priest only on the most weighty grounds.

Here it is instructive to contrast the U.S. Episcopal Church with the Church of England. *The Canons of the Church of England: Canons Ecclesiastical Promulgated by the Conventions of Canterbury and York in 1964 and 1969* contain a "Proviso to Canon 113 of the Code of 1603."[10] This canon is the classic statement that a confession to a Church of England priest is always to be kept confidential by the priest unless his doing so would place the priest's own life in danger. It is thus a *canon* in the English church, and its wording is comparable to the *rubric* associated with the rite of reconciliation in the 1979 U.S. Prayer Book. The canons in the English church do apparently have, with the rubrics of the English Prayer Book, the force of law in England inasmuch as the Church of England is the established church in that country and inasmuch as prayer book rubrics and ecclesiastical law were formally given that force by an act of Parliament, the 1662 Act of Uniformity. The Canon 113 Proviso in the latest promulgation of English church canons, in any case, would seem to pertain to bona fide religious confessions, as does the U.S. prayer book rubric. Even in England, however, Canon 113 has apparently not been used successfully against a legal order that a cleric provide testimony in a court of civil law. Sir William Dale writes that

> the law relating to the Church of England, called the ecclesiastical law, is part of the general law of England, and the clergy and the laity (so far as it applies to the latter) are subject just as much to it as to any other part of the law. But it is enforced by special courts, the ecclesiastical courts, though to some extent also by the ordinary courts of law.[11]

Dale cites the 1736 British case of *Middleton v. Crofts* (2 Atk. 650) in which Lord Hardwicke decided that the 1603 canons "do not *proprio vigore,* that is, as canons of convocation, bind the laity. But as far as they were merely declaratory of the ancient canon law, and did not introduce new matter, they embody rules which are binding on the laity."[12]

The situation changes drastically, however, when a church in communion with the Church of England explicitly places itself outside the authority of legal establishment, as did the Episcopal Church in the United States and, more recently, the church in Wales, which was "disestablished" by the Welsh church acts of 1914 to 1945. By these acts, "the ecclesiastical courts of Wales are to cease to exercise jurisdiction, and, most important of all, the ecclesiastical law of Wales is to cease to exist as law."[13] Dale remarks, "This means, amongst other things, that the church in Wales may settle its own forms of worship without seeking an Act of Parliament."[14] From a legal point of view, the church in Wales appears to resemble the U.S. Episcopal Church more than it does the Church of England, with respect to its autonomy in formulating canons and liturgy.

In the United States, disestablishment was never an issue in the significant way it was in Wales, owing to the different historical situations resulting from the American Revolution. Thus in America in 1782, William White's *The Case for the Episcopal Churches in the U.S. Considered* proposed "a comprehensive plan for the organization of the church on a federal pattern," largely as it came to be accomplished at the first General Convention in 1789. White proposed an autonomous, united, national church structure "independent of all foreign, civil, or ecclesiastical jurisdiction, and entirely separate from national and state control."[15] White met with representatives of the Pennsylvania churches two years later and with them adopted a set of "Fundamental Principles" proclaiming the Episcopal Church's "independence . . . from all foreign authority and its full and exclusive power to regulate" its own concerns.

An Episcopal Church assembly in Annapolis, Maryland, fashioned a similar "Declaration of Fundamental rights and liberties," which was signed on August 13, 1783. The declaration was then reaffirmed in Chester, Maryland, in October 1784. The statement makes explicit reference to "the constitution and form of Government of this state" (i.e., Maryland) and its "Civil Independence." It affirms that the Episcopal Church is "independent of every foreign or other Jurisdiction." Only with respect to the "continuance of the . . . Three Orders of Ministers forever" was any connection allowed to the Church of England. The "Final Principle" declares the Protestant Episcopal Church's "Right" and "Duty" to "revise her Liturgy, Forms of Prayer, and public Worship, in order to adopt the same to the late Revolution and other local circumstances of America. . . ."[16]

The Maryland document with the Pennsylvania document and the personal influence of William White combined to make the liturgical and canonical independence of the U.S. church an accomplished fact at the 1789 Convention of the Episcopal Church. This first General Convention adopted a constitution essentially outlined by the Maryland and Pennsylvania assemblies.[17] In it, neither the English Canons of 1603 nor the Parliament's Act of Uniformity of 1662, which gave the rubrics of the English Prayer Book the force of law in England, have any standing or consequence for the U.S. Episcopal Church.

That the U.S. Episcopal Church was first accountable to itself rather than the Church of England in matters legal and ceremonial was further underscored by the new church constitution's ratification process. This specified the need for approval by the Episcopal Church in the various states in America, decidedly not by anyone in England.

Thus, one finds this in the preface to the 1979 U.S. *Book of Common Prayer.*

But when in the course of Divine Providence, these American States became independent with respect to civil government, their ecclesiastical independence was necessarily included; and the different religious denominations of Christians in these States were left at full and equal liberty to model and organize their respective Churches, and forms of worship, and discipline, in such manner as they might judge most convenient for their future prosperity; consistently with the constitution and laws of their country. (P. 10)

The prayer book preface, written by the Reverend Dr. William Smith for the proposed book of 1786, has appeared in every edition of the American Prayer Book. The same preface goes on to assert the Episcopal Church's legal, canonical "ecclesiastical independence" from England, yet states that as a church it otherwise remains in communion with England's national church.

It is evident that the English canon has not been adopted by the U.S. church as a canon; nor has any act of the U.S. government given the Episcopal Church's prayer book rubrics the force of law. What has happened in England since the founding of the Episcopal Church in the United States is different from what has happened here. The Episcopal Church differs, with respect to law, from the Church of England *predominantly* because it is a nonestablished church and has established its own laws.

Rubrics as Ceremonial Directions

According to the *Oxford Dictionary of the Christian Church* (cited above) rubrics are "ritual or ceremonial directions, printed at the beginning of service books, or in the course of a text. . . ."[19] *The Westminster Dictionary of Liturgy and Worship* concurs: Rubrics are "ceremonial directions."[20] *A New Dictionary for Episcopalians* by the Reverend John Wall, Jr., agrees: "Rubrics are directions found in the prayer book about the conduct of worship."[21] Yet one sometimes hears U.S. clergy announce that, even apart from the Church of England, the U.S. prayer book rubrics have the force of law. Is it so? There is no authoritative statement to that effect anywhere. Those few authorities proposed as warranting such an inference include article 10 of the Episcopal Church's constitution. This article, however, only places the Prayer Book "in use in all the Dioceses of this church." There is, in fact, no indication of a *rubric* possessing the force of law. One searches further, turning to E.A. White and J.A. Dykman's *Annotated Constitution and Canons for the Government of the Protestant Episcopal Church in the U.S.A., Otherwise*

Known as the Episcopal Church.[22] It provides an "exposition of Article 10" on pages 132 and following. This source explains that the issue addressed by article 10 is the American church's need, following the Revolution, to be appropriately similar to, yet different from, the Church of England—particularly respecting the consecration of bishops. Such was the only concern underlying article 10. The rubrics are part of the Prayer Book, and the Prayer Book contains the Episcopal Church's standard of regular worship. But that is the extent of the matter.

Another possible source of support for rubrics as law is title 2, canon 3, of the national canons. This specifies that a priest may be tried in a church court for violating a prayer book rubric. A cursory reading of this canon might appear to support the inference that since one can be tried in a church court for violating a rubric, then a rubric can function enough like a law that we should accord it the force of law. But the difficulty is that rubrics are not the same thing as law, as was shown above; rather, they are ceremonial directions. Moreover, in the main they function differently from laws—though they share with laws the one property, arguably, of being actionable if they are violated. Does this single characteristic provide sufficient foundation to support the gravity and solemnity essential to the case for rubrics having the force of law? Perhaps yes, if we had church trials for people who violate rubrics. These would make us urgently mindful of our need to kneel while saying the general confession in Morning Prayer I, lest we be prosecuted for only sitting. But common sense and our experience remind us that people are not in fact prosecuted for violating rubrics. We also find it difficult to reconcile such prosecutions with the Gospel of Christ, with the broad Anglican heritage, or with a community founded on trust and love. So the canon seems odd; it calls attention to itself as an ill-fitting piece of the church's apparatus. It asks for our investigation into its origins. What could this canon possibly have meant? What was its intent? Its function? What problem was it designed to solve?

Again one consults White and Dykman. Their authoritative history of this canon as it pertains to rubrics recounts the disastrous and since discredited attempt by some in the 1871 General Convention, meeting in Baltimore, to establish uniformity in the ritual conduct of the eucharist precisely by according to rubrics the force of law.

In 1871, the House of Deputies' Committee on Canons thought

that to bend the rubrics toward law was "unwise and inexpedient." The deputies instead asked the House of Bishops to respond to a conflict over the appropriate way to celebrate the Lord's Supper by proposing "such additional rubrics on the Book of Common Prayer as in their judgment may be deemed necessary"—rubrics precisely, rather than canons. The bishops declined to do even this but did appoint a committee to further study the issue of uniformity in ritual as a possible matter of canon law. This bishops' committee ended up proposing the regulation of ritual by the force of law, prohibiting by law such things as "the use of incense," "carrying a cross in procession in the church," "the mixing of water with the wine as part of the service, or in the presence of the congregation," and the like.[23] The effect of this upon the 1871 Convention was to fuel an already growing controversy.

The bishops as a whole declined to act on the recommendations of their own committee. They instead asked that the House of Deputies participate in further hearings regarding ritual uniformity through a joint committee of deputies and bishops. The resulting joint committee then came up with still different proposals in a convention by then in uproar. There were numerous proposals for canons governing ritual, all of which were defeated.

The matter was left, in 1871, with two resolutions. The first simply condemned "all ceremonies, observances and practices which are fitted to express a doctrine foreign to that set forth in the authorized standards of this church."[24] The second ducked the issue of rubrics being converted into canons by leaving matters of ritual solely in the hands of the bishops and their "pastoral counsel and advice." The sum of the matter was that, having faced squarely the question of making ritual and rubrics a matter of canon law, the 1871 Convention found that it could not do so. (Appropos of the confessional issue, it is interesting to note that after the 1871 Convention ended, the House of Bishops sent a pastoral letter strongly condemning auricular confession, along with veneration and invocation of the saints and Eucharistic Adoration.[25])

To understand better the context within which attempts were made to give rubrics the force of law it helps to examine the intense controversy surrounding the mid-19th-century Oxford movement in the United States (or the Tractarians or ritualists, as Anglo-Catholics were then called). To be sure, many sincere and devout Anglo-Catholics and evangelicals advocated their beliefs in reasonable ways. But some in each group were unduly partisan, and as a consequence, the Episcopal Church's life was somewhat battered throughout much of the nineteenth century. Issues emerged from the uproar that influenced the Episcopal Church's understanding of confession.

Bishop Hobart, for example, was in 1818 a prominent "high churchman of the Laudian type" who was, however, particularly vehement in opposing auricular confession and private absolution.[26] These he regarded as "an encroachment on the rights of conscience, an invasion of the prerogative of the searcher of hearts."[27] Bishop Alonzo Potter of Pennsylvania, an evangelical, denounced "the blasphemies of Rome . . . our most formidable evil." Seeing the high church advocates as virtual minions of the pope, Potter also blasted "the private confessional, and the sacrament of penance," which promoted "more power and less responsibility for the clergy, and more responsibility and less liberty for the people."[28] Bishop Levi Sillimon Ives of North Carolina, who had graduated from the General Theological Seminary and then married Bishop Hobart's daughter, was a strong advocate of auricular confessions and generally of the high church agenda. He eventually notified Rome, but not the House of Bishops, of his intention to become a Roman Catholic, whereupon the Episcopal bishops deposed him. His questionable actions and judgments as a "high church" partisan brought more discredit upon the high church views, including views on confession, than was perhaps otherwise warranted. The Episcopal Church, in any case, was now entering a period of turmoil.

By the 1860s, the evangelicals in the Episcopal Church were expressing their dissatisfaction with the "regeneration" passages in the baptismal office. Perhaps provoked by this issue, or perhaps falling victim to the overall partisan polarization that was taking place, Presiding Bishop John Henry Hopkins in 1866 published his book *The Law of Ritualism*. In it, Hopkins pronounced that the "liturgical practices of the second year of Edward VI" were, in fact, the legal rituals for the Church of England and that therefore the U.S. ritualists in the Episcopal Church were, not only allowed, but canonically required to use them in this country.[29] This forced the issue in clear and compelling terms. A response was not long in coming. Hopkins's book was answered on January 10, 1867, when a majority of the House of Bishops issued a declaration repudiating the notion that any ritual or canon law from the English Prayer Book was applicable to the

U.S. church with the force of law. In the Episcopal Church, the pot was now boiling, as partisans of ritualism and their adversaries each tried to enshrine their liturgical preferences in church law. The 1874 General Convention heard several memorials asking that canon law govern the church's ritual. At one point the deputies approved a canon, only to have it rejected by the bishops; then vice versa. Finally, a canon was adopted by both houses that allowed a bishop to summon the standing committee to investigate, admonish, or, if necessary, bring to trial any priest who explicitly "during the celebration of holy communion" commenced acts not ordained or authorized by the *Book of Common Prayer* or set forth "erroneous or doubtful doctrines." The examples offered of triable offenses—all occurring within the conduct of the Lord's Supper—included elevating the elements of the table, bowing or genuflecting before the elements, and "all other like acts not authorized by the rubrics of the Book of Common Prayer." The "like acts" in this context clearly pertained to the adoration of the elements. Here was a connection between the violation of a rubric and the risk of trial in a church court, all of which might be sufficient grounds to say, in 1874, that at last some rubrics might carry the "force of law." Yet the particular rubrics were those that pertained to the Holy Eucharist and, more exactly, had to do with the apparent danger of adoring the elements. Even so, despite this curious moment in Episcopal church history, there is no evidence of anyone ever having been tried for violating a prayer book rubric.

By 1904, various zealotries having calmed down, the General Convention simply and quietly dropped the 1874 canon altogether, recognizing its brief tenure instead with a vague statement allowing that a priest might be tried for departing from the prayer book rubrics. White and Dykman are clear in showing that the sole intention of the 1904 canon was to clean up an old unresolved embarrassment regarding the adoration of elements in the service of Holy Communion. Certainly there is no record in the history of this canon that it had anything to do with any aspect of confession. Much more to the point, however, the political furor in the 1871 and 1874 General Conventions hardly supports a claim that rubrics carry the force of law.

To summarize on this particular point: Holding that "rubrics have the force of law" simply doesn't work—both because the considerable weight of evidence shows rubrics to be ceremonial directions, rather than canons, and because the Episcopal Church discovered, to its considerable embarrassment, the dangers of trying to impose the gravity of law upon the conduct of religious ceremony. Indeed, whenever the church has attempted to legislate in matters of ritual or worship, it has appeared foolish, as is evident from the record of the 1871 and 1874 Conventions. Therefore, it is not at all surprising that in *Prayer Book Rubrics Expanded,*[30] published by the Episcopal Church's Church Hymnal Corporation, rubrics are described as occurring in three ways in the 1979 U.S. prayer book:

1. "Normative rubrics," written "generally in the present indicative (examples include "is, reads, stand, sit, kneel" and "shall, is directed, is required" or "be" with the infinitive)

2. "Rubrics which recommend" (such as, "it is customary, it is fitting, it is desirable")

3. "Permissive rubrics," which are generally recognized by the term *may*

The author summarizes his study of rubrics by quoting Canon Charles Guilbert, custodian of the Standard Book of Common Prayer. Guilbert characterizes the prayer book rubrics simply as "descriptive, not prescriptive." Reasonable people, therefore, might be persuaded that attempts to give rubrics the force of law by actually making them *into* law could carry the church beyond the notorious difficulties of legislating morality toward the even greater difficulties of legislating aesthetics.

As applied to confidentiality, which the "Reconciliation of a Penitent" rubric patently enjoins, the salient fact remains that, as a matter of law (according to a "Memo on Privileged Communications in the Episcopal Church"), "there are no provisions in either the constitution or the canons . . . dealing with this subject."[31] This document, generated by the Executive Council of the Episcopal Church, simply states the plain truth. The best basis upon which to enjoin a priest not to divulge a confidence learned in the conduct of the prayer book rite "Reconciliation of a Penitent" is simply that good faith, mutual respect, and a reasonable pledge of secrecy based upon personal and professional integrity require that we honor our word. There may, of course, be some things more important than the pledge of secrecy, and these might override that pledge in certain circumstances. These, however, would constitute the instances of remarkable exception to the general rule.

4

Pastoral Counseling: Confidentiality versus the Duty to Divulge, the Duty to Care, and Others

In the previous chapter, I discussed one way the clergy interact with parishioners—through religious confession. This entails a clergy professional performing an explicitly religious function, where "sin" in one or more of its various aspects is clearly recognized and acknowledged by the parties. Here the penitent's need for reconciliation to God and the community raises the prospect of absolution. A special kind of strict confidentiality is implied. The term *seal* is an apt indicator of the inviolability of that confidentiality.

Let us now look at counseling in general. The expressly religious and sacerdotal aspects of sin, forgiveness, and restoration to God and God's Church are not in central focus. General pastoral counseling—which includes problem solving, relationship mending, and perhaps even matters of criminal offense—may well involve discussions of sin, aspects of religion, and the like. But in pastoral counseling, the secular issues are explicitly in focus, not necessarily the religious ones. The present chapter considers the limited issue of breach of confidentiality within the context of pastoral counseling in general.

Some clergy will likely be faced with a situation similar to this: A fifteen-year-old boy has ingested a drug that causes him to experience a "bad trip," with acute anxiety, hallucinations, and other symptoms. He calls you on the telephone, announcing that he intends to harm himself. He refuses to tell you where he is unless you promise "solemnly" to keep the entire matter in confidence. Taking everything into consideration, you decide to promise "absolute confidentiality" as he requests. You reason that you will at least be able to get to this boy, and you hope you will then be able to persuade him to let you help him—even if this should require a subsequent waiver of confidentiality. You learn of his location and find him. He is, indeed, in a severely agitated state of mind, but he refuses to release you from your promise of confidentiality. Now you must weigh your promise of confidentiality in the light of this boy's danger to himself, and you consider the possibility that you have an overriding duty to divulge the truth to others who can help him. What do you decide, and how do you do it?

Or suppose that in this sort of case the boy does not intend to harm himself, but he does intend to run away from home "this very night." Would this modification in the story change your way of thinking about confidentiality versus divulgence? Now suppose the person were not a fifteen-year-old boy but a fifteen-year-old girl intending to run away. Would this change your thinking or your decision in any way?

Suppose that the person were thirty-five years old, seemingly intent upon harming himself or herself. Given the same set of circumstances as indicated above, to which duty would you assign a higher value: to keep the confidence or, for the sake of the individual's health and safety, to seek other assistance, even when doing so requires a breach of the confidentiality you have promised?

Or, in somewhat less of an urgent emergency, suppose you have counseled Rosemary Smith for enough time to know that she is in some sense sociopathic. That is, you know Smith to be a person of great skill in conning other people, and you also know that she is usually engaged in nefarious and financially perilous business endeavors. Smith tells you that she is engaged to a wealthy and recently widowed parishioner many years older than she. You believe that the entire situation is a replica of many others in Smith's sordid past. Smith refuses to disclose to her fiancé her marital history or anything about her financial history. Moreover, she holds you to your promise of confidentiality. This, you believe, makes you an unwilling party to the fraud and eventual financial ruin of Smith's fiancé. You object to being silenced by confidentiality. You insist on your positive moral duty to warn your parishioner—the fiancé—whom you see as a lonely, bereaved, and therefore easily victimized target. Smith, however, holds you to your prior pledge of confidentiality. What is your decision and why?

Good faith and common sense, and indeed an acute ethical sensitivity, may in certain circumstances oblige us to divulge certain things said in confidence, whether they are said within the context of the church's pastoral counseling or outside it— though, to be sure, almost all things said in confidence to clergy in any context will probably be forever sealed. But a clergy person is better prepared for tough decisions if he or she has at least considered the "duty to divulge" and a few of the instances in which that duty *may* be overriding.

Clergy Having Knowledge of Possible Child Abuse

The question as to the reach of confidentiality is a complex one. For example, I investigated child abuse and neglect for a three-year period as a state employee. During that time I regarded myself as entirely respectful of people's desires for confidentiality. During the same period of time I felt entirely respectful, too, of the separation of church and state and the room such separation makes for clergy confidentiality.

An instance arose in which a religious sect was discovered to be moving their young children from one community to a distant community where another group of the same sect lived. There those children were forcibly employed as free labor in hideous conditions inside a sect-owned meat-packing plant. I was responsible for investigating that case, and I sought evidence voluntarily and energetically from the clergy leadership of that sect for the district attorney's charges of involuntary servitude of those children. The sect leaders, for their part, attempted to suppress evidence on the ground of clergy confidentiality, privilege, and the notion that their activities were protected by the free exercise clause of the First Amendment. Within the exigencies of that situation, however, the plight of the exploited children seemed much more a cause of concern than any issues of clergy confidentiality. It seemed to me that confidentiality, privilege, and free exercise—terms which I shall explicate subsequently—were invoked cynically and harmfully—though I accept the validity of such principles in themselves.

Is it morally acceptable that clergy should possess a blanket right to confidentiality—a right that overrides the duty of a state to protect its own children? Is it acceptable that a priest could be aware of a three-year-old child locked in a closet most of her life by her parents and that this same priest would feel under no moral constraint to intervene on that child's behalf, because doing so should necessitate a breach of confidentiality? These are the sorts of child abuse cases in which an increasing number of states are proclaiming by statute that even clergy have a duty to report and that this duty overrides the clergy-communicant privilege. There are complex issues of both law and morality here. The child abuse instances are useful for clarifying the issues in the gray border of confidentiality, near its outer limits. Such cases are important to examine, not least because children as a class have such limited access to society and clergy sometimes have knowledge of abusive family situations.

An exchange of views in the *Christian Century* magazine from February through June 1986 nicely brings out the arguments among church people in the matter of confidentiality and divulgence with respect to child abuse. The initial presentation was made by Jeffery Warren Scott, whose argument was that state laws requiring clergy to report known or even suspected instances of child abuse or neglect are objectionable for a number of reasons. First among these is that such laws may seriously diminish the likelihood that a priest can deal beneficially with the presumed perpetrator of abuse. Scott seemed to appeal to the probability that a perpetrator who feels betrayed would not continue in a constructive counseling relationship with someone he or she regarded as a betrayer. (Among the unstated assumptions here is that the one betrayed is either best treated or only treated by the pastor. Another is that the sort of counseling undertaken voluntarily with clergy is, in the case of child abuse, likely to be as effective as, or more effective than, the court-supervised kind. Both these assumptions are debatable.)

Another of Scott's objections to the mandatory reporting of child abuse was that the person reported may go on to express his or her rage at the expense of the child. (Protective services professionals, however, report no instances of this occurring, nor is there social science documentation in support of this fear. To the contrary, all the available indications are that alleged perpetrators of child abuse become more careful not to hurt their children *precisely* because they have been brought under public scrutiny by a report to state authorities.)

Scott's third objection was the "constitutional" objection—that the state's requirement that clergy report known or suspected child abuse intrudes upon a First Amendment right guaranteeing the free exercise of religion. (The assumption here is that the exercise of religion includes the right to ignore, if necessary, the police powers of the state when they might otherwise be invoked to protect an endangered child. There are many who would find this assumption objectionable.)

Another of Scott's objections to mandatory reporting was that, by failing to protect a perpetrator's confidence, the Church will discourage people from receiving counseling, sacramental absolution, or both. Still another objection was that, if clergy can be compelled by the state to divulge child abuse communications, then the state may find it easier to drive a wedge even further into confidential church matters. Scott argued, therefore, that churches and their clergy should hold the line against legally compelled divulgence of confidences, even with respect to possible child abuse.

By April, a number of readers had responded to Scott's article, most of them taking issue with it. One correspondent wrote that she had been sexually abused by a minister who had been counseled by her father, also a pastor. She stated that her father had kept the entire business confidential, much to her consternation and continuing anguish. This correspondent wondered if Scott were appropriately mindful of the need in pastoral counseling to help counselees see clearly the gravity of what they have done and perhaps were still doing. She also wondered if Scott was appropriately considerate of the child victims and their needs; and she didn't see how reporting child abuse in particular compromised the church's confidentiality in general. In conclusion, she remarked that, since the world is imperfect (hence, the need for confessions of sin in the first place), we cannot have the kind of absolutes that justify an absolute right to total confidentiality in every case.

Other correspondents questioned Scott's chief concern for the perpetrator, rather than the child. They wondered about the sacred trust not so much between pastor and perpetrator as between pastor and child. They challenged the notion that clergy are adequately equipped to deal effectively with the complex factors that bring about child abuse in the first place, and they charged that the continuation of child abuse is more likely when it is *not* reported than when it is. Finally, they noted the fact that time-honored exceptions, even in the most traditional understandings of confidentiality, are made in the case of ongoing crimes.

An article by Marie M. Fortune of the Seattle Center for the Prevention of Sexual and Domestic Violence appeared in June 1986 in the *Christian Century*. Fortune pointed to the "larger ethical context" within which a possible breach of confidentiality ought always to be considered. She suggested that a priest ought to give careful thought to divulging confidences when innocent people stand to be hurt or other grave crimes are being perpetrated. Fortune asked about the priest's legal status as a possible party to a crime of which he or she has had secret knowledge. She wondered about the possible moral duty of a Christian to protect the innocent—in this case innocent children. She went on to say that although there are several commendable reasons why clergy should keep confidences, none of these is designed to enable perpetrators to evade personal responsibility for their actions. Indeed, "shielding people from the consequences of their behavior is likely to endanger others and only postpone the act of repentance that is needed."[1]

Confidences and General Crimes of Neglect

The business of criminal negligence, medical neglect, and other sorts of child endangerment (which is not necessarily about issues of confidentiality) has entailed the use of religion as a shield. The "free exercise of religion" has not, for example, prevented criminal indictments against Christian Science parents in instances of alleged negligent homicide and felony child abuse. Six such charges regarding the deaths of Christian Science children are currently active, the most recent involving John and Katherine King, whose twelve-year-old daughter died of bone cancer in Phoenix, Arizona.[2] Some states take temporary custody of Jehovah's Witness children for the purpose of authorizing needed blood transfusions, and this practice has been upheld repeatedly in courts of civil law. The presumption of free exercise of religion as a warrant for medical neglect of Witness children by parents has consistently failed in court. In a similar vein, a state appeals court has upheld an Oklahoma couple's conviction for manslaughter in the pneumonia death of their three-month-old son. The family belonged to the Church of the First Born, which counseled them to withhold medical treatment of the child.[3] (Besides the state's interest in protecting children, there is another related legal factor. The possibility that a state would extend an exemption to parents of a particular religious faith, allowing them to refrain from obtaining appropriate health care for their children, would probably involve a special, and perhaps unconstitutional, governmental endorsement of that religion. This would be in conflict with the First Amendment's "establishment" clause prohibiting such endorsement.)

Parents are simply not authorized by the free exercise of religion to endanger their children's health or welfare. Indeed, the case is much stronger that parents have a positive duty to protect their children by ensuring that they receive essential health care services when these are needed. The state's interest in the welfare of children is aptly conveyed by the legal term *parens patriai*. According to this, the state presumes to protect children in instances where these parents cannot, or will not, act. Unquestionably, the state will invoke its child protective powers against parents only with the greatest caution. But the fact is that the state's power is clearly there to encroach upon the presumed free exercise of religion when the health and safety of children are at issue.

The above are the major issues that have surfaced in the debate for and against overriding clergy-communicant confidentiality in the instance of reporting known or suspected child abuse. Child abuse and child neglect (medical or otherwise) are matters of criminal law. The case is strong for requiring clergy to report known or suspected instances of child abuse or neglect for all the reasons given and for the additional reason that children constitute the group having by far the fewest civil rights in society. Children are the group of people most isolated from society's protections and resources. Since their social vulnerability is so great, they are entitled to the most strenuously offered protections possible under the law. Given all this, a state's duty to protect its children might arguably be greater than its duty to protect clergy confidences or "freedom of religion" in cases where children are at risk for abuse. (One wonders how strongly clergy would cleave to the inviolability of confidentiality or the sanctity of "freedom of religion" if these were repeatedly invoked in a way allowing clergy to be beaten or neglected.)

Clergy Confidentiality and Civil Litigations

Having considered the issue of divulgence in matters of criminal import, it might be useful now to regard clergy confidentiality within the context of civil litigation. As a matter of law, most states locate the ownership of the clergy-communicant privilege in the communicant only, such that a pastor may not claim the privilege of confidentiality in court if the communicant has waived it. Some states, however (including California, Illinois, and Alabama), give the confidentiality privilege to the clergy as well as to the communicants, so that even if the latter waive their privilege a pastor may still claim it for himself or herself.

In New York, the Reverend Richard W. Reifsnyder, a Presbyterian clergyman, was subpoenaed to testify in a civil divorce proceeding as to what he had been told in confidence in the course of marriage counseling. The clergyman, through his lawyer, attempted to quash the subpoena, arguing that though the divorcing couple once in court had waived their right to confidentiality, he should be allowed to refuse to divulge what he had been a party to in confidence.[4] Reifsnyder believes that it is unfair that the confidentiality privilege should reside in the communicant/counselee alone. He believes that being able to claim the privilege for themselves enables parishioners to have a higher degree of trust in the clergy than otherwise and that this is desirable. Reifsnyder also believes, however, that compelled clergy testimony could force public scrutiny of information that could be hamrful to innocent third parties such as children and that, therefore, clergy should also hold the privilege for themselves. Reifsnyder also argued that when he agreed to enter into marriage counseling with the couple, their mutual agreement was to keep everything between them in confidence. He objected to a subsequent, unilateral waiver by one of the parties. The pastor's beliefs and arguments mattered little, however. The New York court ruled that since the New York statute vested the confidentiality privilege in the communicants/counselees only and since these had waived their rights, the minister must testify as to what he knew. (Such finally did not occur but only because the wife subsequently revoked her waiver.)

Here the legal matter is clear: When a clergy person does not, in fact, possess a statutory privilege, his or her testimony may be compelled in court. Once under court order to testify, the clergy person nonetheless may conscientiously refuse on moral grounds to comply with the court order. In this case, he or she should be prepared to be cited for contempt and perhaps go to jail. Usually, but not always predictably, a jail sentence will not be imposed, or if it is, it may be for only a brief period of time.

It should be evident after considering cases that involve the health and safety of children (or adults), child abuse and neglect, cases of possible fraud and victimization, and the straightforward court-ordered compulsion to testify that the duty to divulge may be powerful in certain instances and sometimes even overriding. The psychological and spiritual efforts expended by clergy in arriving at an appropriate decision are enormously costly for the most conscientious among them. I believe that an *easy* response one way or the other (to keep a confidence or to divulge) is almost never forthcoming and that one suffers doubts no matter the final decision. The nice thing about being a Christian, however, is that *after* we have wrestled as diligently as possible with a given dilemma—which means we have applied the most careful and meticulous commitment to it possible—we know that we are, and have always been, miserable sinners. But thank God, we are forgiven miserable sinners.

Other Overriding Duties? The Nally Case

Not only may clergy have a duty to divulge, which is stronger than a duty to keep a confidence; the clergy may also have other overriding duties as well. These duties may in certain instances override confidentiality. In certain states, they might include a duty to do whatever is necessary to prevent a suicide and perhaps a duty to refer a deeply disturbed person to an appropriate mental health professional. These moral and legal issues were at the heart of the most widely publicized clergy malpractice case in recent times. The process of the civil lawsuit and the ultimate opinion of the California Supreme Court are instructive for our present purposes. The case in its essential detail is as follows.

Kenneth Nally, twenty-four years old at the time of his death (by self-inflicted gunshot wound in April 1979), had been a counselee of the clergy staff at Grace Community Church in the San Fernando Valley area of Los Angeles. In addition to this counseling, Kenneth Nally had been seen by a number of psycho-therapists since 1968. He also had seen a psychiatrist close to the date of his suicide. Further, Kenneth Nally allegedly had made an unsuccessful suicide attempt in March 1979, shortly before visiting the clergy counselors, and was therefore known by them to be possibly suicidal.

In 1980, the parents of Mr. Nally sued Grace Church for one million dollars, claiming that the clergy counselors had known Nally to be dangerously depressed and suicidal and therefore had an overriding duty to involve mental health professionals in his case. They regarded it as negligent that the church counselors did not do so. They alleged also that the clergy had a duty to inform them of their son's precarious state and that, moreover, the counseling given Nally was of a harmful nature to him, aggravating his condition and contributing to his suicide. The church's position was that the Grace Church clergy were validly practicing their First Amendment rights concerning the free exercise of religion; that Kenneth Nally as an adult voluntarily chose to avail himself of Grace Church's counseling; that it is not the business of civil courts to inquire into the nature or extent of church counseling; and that, furthermore, there is no valid basis for regarding secular psychotherapy as a more competent alternative than the church's pastoral counseling, either in Nally's case or any other.

The suit had been twice dismissed, partly on First Amendment grounds (free exercise of religion). However, Kenneth Nally's parents successfully appealed these dismissals to the California District Court of Appeals in Los Angeles, which in a split (2–1) decision ruled that "established principles of California law impose a duty of due care on those who undertake a counseling relationship with suicidal individuals."[5] The appeals court ruled in October 1987 that the Nally case could indeed be brought to trial on grounds of "negligent failure to prevent suicide and intentional or reckless infliction of emotional injury causing suicide."[6] The instance of possible clergy negligence in a sequence of events culminating in suicide was apparently regarded by the appeals court as of greater importance than clergy-communicant confidentiality—at least in the sense that negligence would be taken to include the clergy's failure to breach confidentiality if necessary to notify a professional psychiatrist of Nally's condition. This would have been implied by the clergy's duty of "due care."

Grace Church appealed the appeals court opinion to the California Supreme Court, which in January 1988 unanimously agreed to decide whether or not the church and four of its clergy can be tried on charges of negligence.

Chiefly at issue here, within the scope of this present writing, was whether or not in law clergy prerogatives, including but not limited to confidentiality—even within the explicit context of pastoral counseling—may be sufficient to override certain other concerns. These concerns may include the possibility that some activities occurring behind a shield of clergy prerogative might be dangerous, reckless, or incompetent. The California appeals court held open the possibility that Grace Church clergy had a "duty to divulge"—to a psychiatrist—what they knew about Kenneth Nally and that this duty overrode certain other rights or duties in the case. That the clergy of Grace Church did not assume this duty, said the court, constituted possible grounds of negligence upon which they may be tried.

The consumer protection duty of a state is well established and helps to explain the state's possible role in certain instances. One lawyer put it this way:

> First Amendment protection is not absolute and inviolate but is subject to being outweighed by the state's duty to protect its citizens. The clergy's First Amendment protection, therefore, cannot be used to subvert the state's duty. Furthermore, the Amendment, as expressed in state codes, has been construed as limiting its protection to the purely ecclesiastical and sacerdotal functions of the clergy.[7]

Ordinary pastoral counseling may not be one of those pure functions.

The courts in various states have tended to allow First Amendment privileges in instances where the "free exercise of religion" was closely related to ecclesiastical situations and religious *beliefs;* they have tended to take a much less tolerant view of *actions* based upon those beliefs, especially as those actions might pose a threat to the health, property, morals, and safety of the citizenry. If *pastoral counseling* were a commonly understood, clearly delineated term or if counseling were done by clergy only, a stronger case conceivably could be made for keeping such counseling, and the actions issuing directly from it, within the First Amendment protections as a uniquely religious practice. Church-based counseling may not always and everywhere be regarded as a purely religious matter, however. With respect to counseling in general, states have taken a well-established interest along consumer protection lines, requiring counselors to be licensed after complying with certain minimum quality-control standards. With the state intending to protect people from incompetent secular counseling, there seems to be at least a possibility that the state may take an interest in clerical counseling as well. It may prove increasingly difficult in the years to come to use the First Amendment in general, or clergy confidentiality in particular, as a comprehensive shield against assuming other duties, including the duty to divulge, especially when harm may come to a counselee.

Construing Competing Duties:
The California Supreme Court on Nally

On November 23, 1988, the California Supreme Court handed down its judgment in the Nally case.[8] With Chief Justice Malcolm M. Lucas writing for the court, it was held that "pastoral, nontherapist counselors had no duty to refer a potentially suicidal person to a professional therapist, and thus could not be held liable in negligence following the person's suicide." Justice

Marcus Kaufman and Allen Broussard concurred with the final decision of the court but filed a separate opinion with respect to the duties of the clergy involved. The court's opinion, in the majority and minority, is helpful to our present purpose.

In California law, proving "negligence" requires a plaintiff to demonstrate that a clergy person (in this case) possessed a duty to use care, that the clergy person failed to do that duty, and that an injury resulted from such failure. Citing the California Code of Civil Procedure 377, the plaintiffs had charged that "negligence and outrageous conduct" together constituted "clergyman malpractice," which was actionable in the civil lawsuit.

The supreme court held that "one is ordinarily not liable for actions of another and is under no duty to protect another from harm, absent special relationships of custody or control"—which came to mean specifically and solely a physician's duty to prevent the suicide of a hospitalized patient. The court went on to say that "pastoral, nontherapist counselors" had "no special relationship with a person over whose environment they had no control." Therefore, religious counselors have no duty to prevent a suicide, said Justice Lucas. (Lucas also denied "outrageous conduct" by the Grace Church clergy.)

The supreme court reversed the appeals court in upholding instead the trial court's decision that in this particular case the evidence presented by the Nallys was "insufficient to permit a jury to find in his [their] favor." Of interest is the trial court's remark that "there is no compelling state interest to climb the wall of separation of church [and state] and plunge into the pit on the other side that certainly has no bottom." The trial court had also noted that even if the clergy had a "duty to refer," the evidence in this case failed to show that such duty had been breached.

The interesting question taken up by Justices Kaufman and Broussard, against the supreme court majority, was whether or not, in the first place, a clergy person ordinarily has a legal "duty to care." The framework within which Kaufman and Broussard developed their view is along the following lines: The law says that "a tort, whether intentional or negligent, involves a violation of a legal duty, imposed by statute, contract or otherwise, owed by the defendant to the person injured. Without such a duty, any injury is *damnum absque injuria*—injury without wrong."[9] The supreme court's Nally opinion cites cases requiring the plaintiff to show that the defendant indeed had a duty to use due care and that the defendant specifically had a duty to protect another from harm. The supreme court found, however, that only physicians responsible for hospitalized patients had such a duty in California. The Lucas opinion of the California Supreme Court was based upon the prospect that imposing upon clergy a positive duty to refer pastoral counselees to professional therapists "could deter those most in need of help from seeking "the counsel of clergy." Lucas further wrote that since the California legislature has exempted clergy from the licensing requirements that apply to domestic counselors and psychologists who specialize in marriage, family, child, and domestic issues, the legislature "has recognized that access to the clergy for counseling should be free from state imposed counseling standards." Citing Ericsson, "Clergyman Malpractice: Ramifications of a New Theory,"[10] Lucas averred that "the secular state is not equipped to ascertain the competence of counseling when performed by those affiliated with religious organizations." Along a similar vein, Lucas questioned whether specifiable pastoral counseling standards could be articulated by the courts and whether the identification of those to whom they would apply could be accomplished successfully: "Because of the differing theological views espoused by the myriad of religions in our state, it would certainly be impractical, and quite possibly unconstitutional, to impose a duty of care on pastoral counselors." As noted above, Lucas, speaking for the court's majority, found that the clergy of Grace Community Church had no duty of care toward Kenneth Nally that obliged them to divulge or refer.

Justices Kaufman and Broussard, while concurring in the supreme court's basic judgment in favor of Grace Church, held a minority view within the court that the church's clergy *did* owe a "minimal duty of care" to Kenneth Nally. They felt that the court's majority was incorrect in holding that no duty existed; but they felt the duty that in their view did exist had, in fact, been met by the clergy in this case. Hence, they supported the majority's final determination, though for a different reason.

Justice Kaufman's reasoning went as follows: Even though the First Amendment prevents the government from "prohibiting the free exercise of religion," conduct based upon religious beliefs "remains subject to regulation for the protection of society."[11] Kaufman noted that in the Nally case the clergy defendants did not deny that their religious beliefs prevented them from making a referral or advising a referral to a professional counselor. Citing *U.S. v. Lee,*[12] in which the court compelled Amish people to violate their religious beliefs in order to participate in the Social Security System, and other cases, Kaufman held that "it is well settled that government may as readily compel religiously prohibited conduct as prohibit religiously motivated acts." Kaufman concluded, "Accordingly, courts, including our own, have determined that religious groups may be held liable in tort for their actions, *even where they occur in the context of religiously motivated counseling"* (my emphasis). Kaufman cites three instances of this: *O'Neil v. Schukardt* (1986), in which a church was found actionable for libel when marriage counseling led to invasion of privacy; *Bear v. Reformed Mennonite Church* (1975), where "shunning" of a former member was shown to interfere in business and marriage relations; and *Carrieri v. Bush* (1966), where the court permitted action against a clergyman for alienation of affections. In the Carrieri case, the court stated, "Good faith and reasonable conduct are the necessary touchstones to any qualified [First Amendment] privilege that may arise from any invited and religiously directed family counseling, assistance, or advice."

Kaufman ended his opinion by announcing that "the governmental interest . . . is compelling." He explained,

> Society's interest in preserving the life of a would-be suicide is as profound as its interest in preserving life generally. To this end, society surely may require a pastoral counselor who invites and undertakes a counseling relationship with an individual in whom he recognizes suicidal tendencies, to advise that individual to seek competent medical care. Thus, I am persuaded, on the facts presented, that defendants owed a minimal duty of care to Nally.

Having thus disagreed with the majority in holding that a duty to care did exist for the Grace Church clergy, Kaufman then added that he was "equally persuaded" that the clergy had, in fact, "fulfilled their duty." Ten years later, on April 3, 1989, the U.S. Supreme Court finally put an end to the Nally case by unanimously refusing to review the matter.

Are There Ethical Duties "Higher" than Legal Duties?

Perhaps the chief question for clergy professionals is whether the California court's majority view, holding that pastoral counselors have no legal duty to care or to refer or to prevent a suicide, should be the standard in terms of professional ethics. There is reason to suppose that professional ethics should be more rigorous than what the law allows in any given state. In other words, if clergy practices are conducted within the bounds of the law only, are these practices *therefore* being performed in accordance with a reasonable standard of ethical conduct within their profession? Or are clergy called to "higher duties," along the lines, perhaps, that proceeded from the court's minority opinion? With respect to confidentiality in particular, a professional ethic that supports such positive duties to care, refer, or prevent a (preventable) suicide will clearly entail the strong possibility of breaching confidentiality in certain cases.

The law itself is an ever-changing thing: therefore, in the future a new case will certainly come before the California courts that may modify the applicable laws in that state. And obviously, other states may decide similar cases differently, so that what is legally specified in one state may be specified differently elsewhere.

5

Ethics and the Limits of Confidentiality

The heart knows some things better than the mind. We are intuitively able to recognize instances when the intellect alone does not equip us to meet the urgent requirements of the moment. An example of this is found in the Grand Inquisitor passage from Dostoyevski's *Brothers Karamazov:* Heretics are being burned, and all the labored philosophy and ethics of the Inquisitor are designed to rationalize this killing as being to the glory of God. But since our hearts are anguished by the scene before us, we do not accept the relevance of the Inquisitor's ethics. The heart knows it is not ethical to execute people who question authority. Although Dostoyevski's scene strikes us today as extreme, we recognize that his point is important.

That some situations are not comprehended by ethics alone is also true with respect to the ethics of confidentiality. To take an extreme example: My knowledge that a homicidal maniac intends to shoot your family cannot remain confidential, even if I initially promised confidentiality to the maniac in question. From both an ethics perspective and from the point of view of common sense, to consider maintaining confidentiality in such an instance seems absurd. It is ludicrous to propose that confidentiality embraces a definitive "there's nothing further that needs to be said" position (given such a pathological and plainly criminal context).

But in considering the limits of confidentiality, one need not contemplate homicidal maniacs only. Take the hypothetical case in which Father Jones innocently promises confidentiality to a presumed counselee. Suppose further that it eventually becomes evident that the counselee's true intent is to enlist Jones's aid in covering up ongoing acts of income tax evasion and other crimes in which a number of other persons are the victims. Suppose still further that Jones is also the rector of the parishioners against whom some of the criminal acts are being perpetrated. Suppose even further still that Jones's options are (1) to maintain his promise of confidentiality, in which case the crimes in question stand a significant chance of continuing, with him a passive and knowing observer, or (2) to recognize a duty of care for the victims as well as a fiduciary duty to protect his parish. This latter duty might also include an implied duty to prosecute those undertaking criminal acts against it. What one eventually decides to do will depend upon a variety of factors, which taken together may well predominate over the one principle of confidence-keeping. Indeed, it is not obvious in this example that the ethics of confidentiality are the only, or necessarily the presiding, consideration.

It is generally assumed that many professionals, including clergy, are obliged to honor confidences. This they usually do apart from the strictly *legal* question of whether or not the confidences in question may be *privileged.* In considering what might lie beyond the reach of confidentiality, we should first review briefly what is usually covered by confidentiality. Confidentiality, according to Sissela Bok's book *Secrets,* is based upon three general ethical premises and one particular premise regarding professional secrets. The chief premise is "individual autonomy over personal information," that is, autonomy over such things as belong to our privacy.[1] But this premise itself is limited by the fact that, practically speaking, we are not able to be entirely private; others make observations about us.

It is limited also by the fact that in the United States a clear, all-encompassing "right to privacy" (or in the well-known words of Judge Thomas Cooley, a right "to be let alone") has not been strongly established in law. Cooley's oft-cited 1879 work on torts regarded privacy as a precious thing to be protected against the sort of battery that libel and slander inflict upon one's emotions and peace of mind. Samuel D. Warren and Louis D. Brandeis, in a famous 1890 *Harvard Law Review* article, took up Cooley's notion in other respects that bore chiefly upon one's being displayed through written publications. Their article has since been a primary reference point for legal and ethical inquiries into issues of privacy.[2]

The courts have been weak in supporting privacy rights in general. The U.S. Supreme Court, in *Katz v. U.S.,* said there is "no general constitutional right to privacy."[3] Six years later the same court stated, in *Roe v. Wade,*[4] that since 1891 the First, Fourth, Fifth, Ninth, and Fourteenth Amendments to the Constitution have been interpreted as warranting certain particular privacy rights bearing upon marriage, family, and procreative matters and that therefore "the right of personal privacy includes the abortion decisions."[5] Yet the same court also held that "the constitution does not explicitly mention any right of privacy."[6] Then in 1977, in *Whalen v. Roe,*[7] the Supreme Court ruled that the Constitution does not allow the physician-patient relationship to be grounded in any absolute right of privacy.

Perhaps the most comprehensive nontechnical treatment of the privacy premise and the clearest in conveying its difficulties and lack of definition, is Richard Hixson's *Privacy in a Public Society.*[8] Hixson's summary remark concerning privacy as an aspect of the priest-penitent relationship shows clearly the tentativeness of a presumed legal right to privacy or a corresponding moral right: "But the promise of the intimate state (i.e., of a priest and confessant confidentiality) is not so much a matter of the right to privacy as it is a matter of understood trust and confidence."[9] The matter of privacy as an aspect of confidentiality is thus affected primarily by the characters of those involved in the confidential relationship, their respect for each other, their goodwill, and the circumstances surrounding their particular endeavor. Thus it makes sense to speak of a privacy *premise,* rather than a privacy *right.*

A second general premise proposed by Bok is the mutual respect that enables us to count upon the loyalty of others to retain our confidences as we reciprocate concerning them. This premise warrants the husband-wife privilege in court, for example, whereby a spouse cannot be compelled to testify against the mate. This, however, is itself a tricky business, for though there is no legal compulsion of a spouse to testify against the other, there may be certain moral reasons that such testimony should be offered anyway. Court records involving sexual abuse of girls by their fathers, uncles, mother's boyfriends, and the like are especially rife with implications of a mother's negligence or tacit complicity in these abuses. Frequently, mothers of sexually abused girls end up contributing indirectly to the exploitation of their daughters, chiefly by failing to take appropriate legal steps. Needless to say, a number of serious ethical questions can be raised about the protections of special relationships, such as that between a husband and wife, when acts of significant moral and/or legal import are shielded thereby.

Bok's third general premise is that an initial promise of secrecy may severely limit our freedom. Our promise predisposes us to honor it, and thus it restricts our range of possible responses. For us to override our promise of secrecy would then require a rigorously derived justification. The philosopher W. D. Ross has made us familar with "prima facie duties." Thus in initially promising confidentiality, we have at least accepted a prima facie duty to honor our pledge. A prima facie duty, however, is one that can be overriden, given sufficient justification for doing so. Perhaps an illustration would be helpful.

A priest friend once conveyed to me a personal experience of counseling that I am modifying now to heighten the confidentiality issue and to protect identities. I present this case, in brief outline, to show how an initial promise of confidentiality was unilaterally broken by the priest. A young man in his early thirties began to come for counseling to this priest, an associate on the staff of a large urban parish. It was understood that all the counseling sessions were confidential. During one of these sessions the man admitted that in years past he had made sexual approaches to a number of boys. The priest felt an obligation toward the boys in the parish—especially the acolytes, over whom this man now had oversight. She also felt an obligation to her own superior, namely, the rector. The counselee refused to release her from their joint covenant of confidentiality, claiming that if he had thought she would disclose anything "this personal," he never would have spoken with her about this issue "or any other that matters." He hinted at the possibility of some kind of reprisal if she divulged to anyone what she knew. She finally announced that she was going to speak with the rector, and this she did. Her reason for doing so was that the magnitude of what she had discovered was such as to give greater weight to her concern about the acolytes, to the potential damage to the parish, and to the need of the rector to know. In short, she felt that her initial promise of confidentiality at the first counseling session, weeks before, entailed only a prima facie duty. She believed that the new information to which she subsequently became privy changed and overwhelmed the original situation altogether. In fact, the new information, she felt, created a new situation entirely beyond the reach of confidentiality.

Was she justified in going to the rector? A simpler response would have been to reason that "a confidence is a confidence," and that's that. Someone who assigns the highest value to rule or duty-based ethics might easily take this position. It could be supported, in fact, by the arguments that, among other things,

(1) honoring such rules is exactly what makes priests priests, and that's why we go to them with our deepest concerns; (2) so far as can be known, none of the church's acolytes have been approached by this man, and there is no objective evidence indicating that they will be; and (3) it is possible that the man's admission is part of a first step in a process leading toward his rehabilitation and that treating it as an administrative problem for the clergy would seriously undermine his chances for recovery. The priest would have accepted the foregoing reasoning as sufficient to bind her to secrecy. But then another element in the story appeared. A pivotal judgment made by this priest, a decision that decisively committed her to discussing the matter with the rector, was that the young man seemed to deny that his love for boys, and its sexual expression, was wrong. To him, the problem was that he lived in an intolerant nation and culture. (Within the context of a "confession," this would mean that the element of contrition was not present. If the information had then come up in a "sealed" confessional context, rather than in a pastoral counseling setting, there would be a question as to whether or not this were a valid, contrition-based confession.)

Now the rector: When he was informed by his assistant, what should he have done? Should he have spoken with the counselee only? Should he have perhaps laid down some strict prohibitions such as resigning from the acolyte supervision position and staying away from all the boys in the parish? Does he have a duty to involve the parish wardens in the discussion, considering that the matter could suddenly become a concern, perhaps a threat, to the entire parish? Does he have a duty to warn parents, especially the parents of the acolytes? (He does not know for a fact whether or not this man has already approached one or more of the acolytes.) In short, what are the various duties of the rector—to his assistant, to the counselee, to the wardens, the vestry, the parish in general, and certain parents in particular? How are these duties sorted out and given relative weights?

For my present purpose, I am content simply to describe the overall dilemma. I want only to illustrate Bok's point that an initial promise of confidentiality necessarily imposes a burden upon us that would not be there otherwise. As to what should be done in this case, by whom, why, and so forth, that is a difficult question. I believe the facts of the particular case—which are too numerous and too subtle to recount—significantly determine our judgments. Every situation is, after all, somewhat unique. Who we are in it, what we see, what we do, and so forth, is based ultimately upon our sense of what is going on. Even if we are strict rule-followers, we have to decide which rule (or rules) applies validly to a particular set of circumstances. This entails a decision concerning what sort of circumstance we have in the first place. How we characterize a given situation, therefore, predisposes us toward one or another set of applicable rules. Our most basic determination will have to do with whether or not confidentiality covers the situation at hand.

Clergy and the Limits of Confidentiality

Bok aggregates her three general premises, named above, as compelling prima facie reasons to keep confidences. She adds, however, the following:

> But of course there are reasons sufficient to override the force of all these premises, as when secrecy will allow violence to be done to innocent persons, or turn someone into an unwitting accomplice in crime. At such times, autonomy and relationship no longer provide sufficient legitimacy. And the promise of silence should never be given, or if given, can be breached.[10]

Here is where Bok takes up the particular duty of professionals to keep silent. This is a duty, she states, commended for its overall usefulness in society. Lawyers, for instance, must be able to keep the confidences of their clients in order to give them the best possible defense; clergy, likewise, because of their useful availability to hear sincere confessions, to counsel, and to absolve people from guilt.

Things would be regarded as working well under this arrangement for professional confidentiality if and when professionals did actually help, rather than hurt, their clients and if and when society were helped as well. Bok recognizes in the instance of clergy confidentiality that, from a faith perspective, there may also be some beneficial ritualistic meaning attached to the practice of religious confession. She insists, though, that such a faith notion by itself adds no further force to the moral argument for clergy confidentiality. Indeed, the aggregated "rationale of confidentiality" may inflate itself and thus serve to thwart needed ethical inquiry altogether, even when such inquiry might be advisable on grounds of justice. When this happens, "confidentiality, like all secrecy, can then cover up for and in turn lead to a great deal of error, injury, pathology, and abuse."[11] The use of confidentiality by professionals as a shield, behind which to carry on practices removed from public scrutiny, can be unjustly self-serving and partly or fully intentional and manipulative. There is for clergy a remarkable amount of latitude for hiding behind a confidentiality shield. In practice, many courts will steer clear of serious challenges to clergy confidentiality simply in order to avoid the time and hassle of a struggle that may not produce results significant to the case at hand. In practice, then, clergy who assert a legal privilege of confidentiality can often succeed in avoiding the scrutiny that would befall others outside their profession. Precisely because of the widespread understanding by clergy that they are, in general, fairly well insulated behind a shield of confidentiality, there is a danger of their slipping into a sense of complacency about morality in general. Sometimes there are few real accountabilities. Thus, it is possible even for professionals trained at, say, the master's degree level in *theories* of ethics and morality to adopt an attitude of ease about the practice of the same. After all, if one can invoke confidentiality at will and get away with it, then one is not forced to account for some of the things others generally might have to account for.

The examples are numerous. They include the moderately harmless deceit called the "pastoral emergency," which is recognized by clergy insiders as the bogus excuse for not attending a boring or inconvenient clergy conference (or if attending it, then leaving early). The pastoral emergency tends to succeed because it is considered to be in bad form for others to inquire into the nature of a pastoral emergency—owing precisely to the pre-sumption that such things are inherently confidential. The announcement of a pastoral emergency, accompanied by the knowing wink, conveys the real message that "I don't want to be here; I'm going to joke my way out of it; and that's all I'm going to say about it!"

Another example, a little more worrisome, is the "everybody does it" response to an impropriety of one sort or another. Since they can generally avoid disclosing improprieties, clergy can eventually become somewhat accepting of them. For example, when a person (whether parishioner or clergy) embarks upon illegal or immoral endeavors, these can end up being regarded as only a "pastoral matter." Or in the case of, say, philandering, a not infrequent "pastoral" response is that "everyone does it" or that "boys, after all, will be boys." Women may take a different view of what seems to them to be a light, pastoral response to the philandering problem. They might make the point that, if discovered, women are not likely to get off so easily (whether women clergy or women laity) and that a little bit of "everybody-does-it" philandering can lead to an awful lot of heartache, because the damage in just one instance can be considerable. In other words, "pastoring" alone does not appear to take appropriate account of the moral dimensions to certain indiscretions. Here, the shield of confidentiality can be a part of the problem. The fact that church authorities of any level may, and do, count on confidentiality tends in its own peculiar way to allow the difficult moral and ethical dilemmas to be obscured or perhaps even avoided because one is instead being "pastoral." The end of such a progression, or perhaps erosion, is that pastoring might become, like patriotism, the last refuge of the clergy scoundrel.[12]

In church contexts where moral and ethical problems tend to be treated only as pastoral problems, there is frequently a tacit collusion by clergy and laity alike that becomes ultimately disrespectful of people, of adult responsibility, of real damage to others, of the truth. A process of this sort is aided by an otherwise commendable and correct (as far as it goes) reluctance to seem malicious or punitive toward someone who has engaged in unethical or illegal practices. Malice and vindictiveness surely have no place in a Christian community. But neither does the deceit that "pastoring" is always and everywhere the adequate and appropriate response to a moral or ethical predicament. Moral transgressions *mean* that a wrong has been committed and that the wrong needs to be set right, if it can be. This heads the matter in the direction of contrition. What, however, sometimes passes for pastoring—though clergy may tend to deny this publicly—is an overemphasis upon psychological techniques and reassurances. The values and norms of Christian conduct, as these appear in the Christian heritage, are available to give breadth and depth to pastoring.

Concerns generally falling into this category have interested Professor Don Browning of the University of Chicago. He has achieved well-deserved acclaim for his investigations into this area in *The Moral Context of Pastoral Care,* published in 1976.[13] His continuation piece is the 1983 *Religious Ethics and Pastoral Care.*[14] In this he states his intent for both works: "Before we can exercise care (or even know what it is) we have to have a religious ethic. . . . The minister doing pastoral care must be an ethical thinker and understand the methods of ethical thinking."[15] Browning devotes an entire chapter to what he calls "the estrangement of care from ethics." Another is devoted to "the movement toward ethical neutrality"—a movement that does not seem entirely sensible since the gospel, and the life of Christ upon which it is based, is anything but neutral.

Cases Involving the Health and Safety of Others

A few other specific instances should be mentioned in which questions concerning the reach of confidentiality might arise. Female minors with problem pregnancies, for example, sometimes present unique problems of health and safety that conflict strongly with physician-patient confidentiality. A clergy person might similarly feel conflicted over confidential information of this sort. Similarly, a young man with AIDS intends to marry a woman and become sexually active with her without telling her of his illness. In cases like these, what obligations fall upon the physicians (or clergy) from whom the patient requires confidentiality? The Council on Ethical and Judicial Affairs of the American Medical Association has recently answered that question for physicians by saying, "Where there is no statute that mandates or prohibits the reporting of seropositive individuals to public health authorities and a physician knows that a seropositive individual is endangering a third party, the physician should (1) attempt to persuade the infected patient to cease endangering the third party; (2) if persuasion fails, notify authorities; and (3) if the authorities take no action, notify the endangered third party."[16]

The National Academy of Science's Institute of Medicine proposed, however, that physicians generally should *not* have a legal duty to notify the sexual partners of HIV-positive people —even if the infected person refuses to do so.[17] The institute questions both the practicality of reaching such partners and the potential such practice would have for inhibiting voluntary testing altogether. The well-respected report of the Presidential Commission on the Human Immunodeficiency Virus Epidemic, chaired by Admiral James Watkins, makes the same suggestion concerning the legal obligations of physicians.[18] This commission unanimously recommended, however, that public health officials (rather than the patient's physician) should act upon a doctor's confidential information to notify a sex partner if the infected person refuses to do so. The commission named eight circumstances in which a person's confidentiality right should be overridden, all pertaining to when the safety of others is seriously threatened. The duties, moral or legal, for clergy having confidential knowledge of situations like these are no less murky than they are for physicians.

A California court held that a psychiatrist has a duty to breach confidentiality in order to warn a potential victim that a patient intended to kill her. Said the state supreme court: "The privilege (of confidentiality) ends when the public peril begins."[19] The court was not persuaded when psychiatrists argued that confidentiality is more overriding than a duty to warn a possible victim. The psychiatrists said that members of their profession are more often incorrect in predicting violent behavior than they are correct. They added that a ready resort to breaching confidentiality in such cases markedly weakens the trust necessary for effective therapy. The counter claim is that even in the unlikelihood that death or severe injury might occur, the stakes are sufficiently high to justify breaking confidentiality to protect the innocent. Further, there is no evidence establishing that therapy will be compromised if patients are warned that a professional is required to divulge certain types of confidences. Still further, the third party (the possible victim) has, it might be held, a right to be consulted in decisions affecting his or her health and safety. A situation of this sort is beyond the reach of the ordinary duty to keep a confidence; in the apt words of the California Supreme Court, confidentiality is a duty that now simply "ends."

Individuals, says Bok, cannot be given autonomy to the extent that they may plan or implement acts of violence against the innocent. Indeed, it is unfair for someone to require that a professional possess information of such a sort in confidence, for to do so may well be to attempt to involve the professional as an accomplice in violence or injustice. It follows from this line of thought that professionals cannot and should not offer a blanket promise of confidentiality even from the beginning. In any case, when serious threats arise against innocent third parties or against the overall good of society, then the professional may be allowed —indeed, may be expected—to be released from the bond of confidentiality. (Whether a professional is *allowed* to breach confidentiality—say, to warn a victim—or, more strongly, is *obliged* to do so, is a matter not considered here in detail. It would seem, however, that the greater likelihood of greater harm moves the moral case for divulgence from permission toward obligation.)

Pathological or Unjust Counseling Relationships

It is reasonable to expect that in most cases professionals will

72

be on strong moral grounds when they honor confidences, keeping secrets from public review. But there are, as here indicated, conflicting duties that compete with confidentiality. Some situations in themselves do not seem tractable in a simple or comprehensive way to the presumed duty of a professional to honor a confidence. All this, so far, is based on the assumption that what passes between the professional and client within the pastoral counseling relationship itself is *more or less* healthy, sincere, and so on. More should be said, however, about those conversations between a clergy person and communicant in which a significant number of complex psychological elements are present—for example, deceit, pathology, intended manipulation, and the like. Here the focus is upon the counseling relationship that in itself is becoming subject to extreme forms of wickedness. Situations of this sort require shrewd judgments by the professional in an area that is murky and occasionally treacherous. As above, one's interpretation of a given conversation as pathological, for example, can determine whether one decides that confidentiality validly covers the situation or not.

The issue is raised implicitly in an article by Morris B. Abram, chair of the President's Commission for the Study of Ethical Problems in Medicine and Bio-medical and Behavioral Research.[20] Abram proposes that physicians enter into a "shared relationship" with their patients, in which treatment decisions are mutually developed. Abram believes that such an approach as this would significantly mitigate the mistrust and ill will that sometimes give rise to medical malpractice suits. It would also tend, he believes, to reduce the pressures upon doctors to practice "defensive medicine," a financially costly recourse that involves ordering unneeded diagnostic procedures. Implicit in Abram's proposal are the presumptions of rationality and good will on all sides. In consideration of a different set of circumstances, however, a physician friend remarks, "We are used to dealing with normalcy, but when it is not there all bets are off." Another unstated premise is that the primary impetus toward litigation is mistrust rather than, say, greed. But greed might well be less tractable to amiable communication than to meticulously practiced "defensive medicine." If a rapacious person decides to sue someone in order simply to get money (which is a primary motive for many suits) the suit will likely occur, *regardless*.

Within the counseling experience of various professionals, including clergy, it is almost axiomatic that elements of psychopathic manipulation can, and frequently do, appear in interview situations. Among counselors of all types it is taken for granted that the counselee "wants" something, whether sympathy, support, or active response to one problem or another; it is also taken for granted that the counselee's principal objective initially determines what is said, what is not said, and how everything comes up. In anticipation of these contingencies, seminary courses and clinical training situations abound in which a primary objective is to help the would-be counselor understand what is really going on beneath or in addition to or instead of what the counselee is simply stating. Lecture, seminar courses, and clinical training are also devoted to the study of manipulative intrusions into the counseling context by the professional himself or herself as well, whether these are conscious, unconscious, or both.

In any counseling situation, both the pastor and the communicant must and usually do make judgments about this other with whom one is in conversation. These judgments are directed not only to the personality but also toward the character of another; they're concerned with his or her basic trustworthiness, prudence, overall emotional health, probity, and so on. And thus when we think about it, we do acknowledge that a competent pastor does not take everything at face value. The pastor, to the contrary, reserves to himself or herself a set of private judgments about the person and circumstances being presented in the counseling situation. These private judgments, by the fact that they exist, demonstrate crucial but hidden elements important in the interpretation of a person and of that person's version of things. It is out of these private judgments that decisions are made, or influenced, concerning confidentiality or divulgence. In very truth, we do make private judgments; we assume responsibility for them; they are as deeply a part of the texture of our lives as is our sometime commitment, based upon prima facie duty, to honor a confidence.[21] Nowhere has it been established that cleaving to a verbal commitment (for example, the promise not to divulge) is always morally preferable to honoring a contrary impulse arising from our private judgments about people or circumstances. Neither is there any possibility that *always* preferring a pledge of confidentiality in conflict situations is either right or good.

Insofar as moral reasoning might be applied to properly characterizing a conversation as "healthy," we might be somewhat reassured if, during that reasoning, we considered the following guidelines:

74

1. What is wanted of me is a fair request, fair enough that I could reasonably make the same request of another if our roles were reversed. (Suppose that I were being asked in confidence to cover up a crime; I would feel that I could not reasonably make that request of another. Therefore, there is an implicit injustice within the confidential situation. My private judgments about that injustice will influence what I do about confidentiality.)

2. I am not being asked to violate my own deepest values.

3. I am not being requested to undertake or become complicit in an action that, if done by anyone else, I would regard as undesirable.

4. What is being asked of me as a pastor allows me to respond in ways compatible with the religious tradition in which I stand. As a priest, responsible to and for the overall well-being of a particular community founded upon and defined within a certain moral and spiritual way of being, I am called upon to conduct myself in a fashion consistent with a particular way of being. As a community of which I am a member, the Church exercises its own values, beliefs, and qualities through me and, of course, through many others as well. This means that I am not entirely free to consider my actions or my being apart from that community of which I am a member. I can and do make independent judgments about people and circumstances, but I do so also within the broad context of the Church's self-understanding and my own self-understanding as one of its members. If a statement is made in confidence to me as a pastor, and if I am allowed to respond in ways fitting to the Church's basic way of being, then I take reassurance in that fact. If, however, a statement comes up in confidence in such a way as to be at odds, or put me at odds, with the Church's basic way of being, then I am forced to make a decision about what I am being asked to do, despite having initially entered into a professional relationship with the counselee where confidentiality was promised or assumed.

One might be helped in understanding this point by considering the issue of reservation about confidentiality in contrast to the issue of lying. Lying is the deliberate intention to deceive another. One whose character has been shaped within a morally conscientious family, or within the Church, might be expected not to lie; he or she would be expected instead to be honest. (Honesty implies a moral integration of intentions, attitudes, behaviors, and the like, with the qualities of truth-telling and respect of persons.) Deliberate concealment of relevant information from another and, perhaps more, the intent to mislead another by active or passive means are inconsistent with honesty: These are lying. Lying is a matter of intent, the intent to deceive. Lying dishonors the other, as it undermines the trust and confidence necessary to human community. Observation suggests that lying has a peculiarly strong way of becoming habitual; it makes us suspicious not only of the liar in this moment but also in any other moment as well.

Truth-telling and confidence-keeping both proceed from a prior commitment to honor self, other, and community. Since confidence-keeping in a way binds me to the confider, it especially requires that this other be of a more or less "honest" character and that the other operate in good faith. My intention to honor this other by limiting myself in the degree appropriate to confidence-keeping is a voluntarily assumed limitation. I accept a burden, which is the confidence, and I limit my freedom on the other's account by limiting what I allow myself to say and do that is related to the confidence. My intention, at bottom, is to honor the other. And yet is it prudent to promise to bear a burden I might not yet adequately know? Is it prudent to enter a special, limited, and limiting relationship with another whose own intentions (and character) I may not adequately know? Prudence might counsel that when asked to keep a confidence, at least in certain circumstances, I should honestly state my intention thus: "I shall try my best to keep confidential what you are about to disclose." My intention would then be clear, honorable, honest. The basis for this or any other statement is my intention to act in good faith, and it presupposes good faith on the part of the other.

Divulgence as Self-Defense

In considering those situations at the limits of confidentiality, or perhaps beyond the reach of confidentiality, I indicate now a class of problems that pose a specifiable array of threats to pastoral counselors or, indeed, to any counselor. These are situations in which a positive threat to the counselor arises within the counseling context. I am not now referring to the attempted seduction of a counselee or to any misbehavior of any sort by a counselor. Nor am I referring to situations of physical danger for either person. I have in mind, instead, instances in which false assumptions, psychological projections, or transferences operate on the part of a counselee in such a way as to pose a danger to the reputation of the counselor. I have in mind, also, the less likely but no less dangerous instance in which a person of questionable motives and personal integrity threatens to slander the counselor by means of false allegations of what was said or done in the absence of third party witnesses (i.e., in an otherwise confidential context). I am concerned, in short, with the vulnerability of a counselor to damage from a counselee—someone either psychologically immature or malicious—when that vulnerability is magnified precisely by confidentiality.

Suppose, for example, you are the Reverend Anne Jones, a wife and mother of two children, on the staff of a large suburban church. Assume also that a man comes to you for counseling, and after a number of counseling sessions indicates to you that he believes you to be in love with him. He remarks that he is about to confide to a few of his acquaintances in the parish that such is the case. In this sort of circumstance, many clergy might feel that their best defense is the truth and that their most promising course of action would be to regard the situation as sufficiently pathological as to cancel the confidentiality duty. Some clergy might attempt to protect themselves by trying to persuade, perhaps coerce, the counselee into seeing a more highly trained counseling professional. But coercion and manipulation are not normally ethically commendable parts of pastoral counseling and in some cases will not work anyway. The Reverend Anne Jones could continue her counseling sessions with the man, but she is not convinced she can get things back into the realm of reality; things could instead get more complicated. She could terminate the counseling relationship and continue for her part to keep whatever was said confidential. Alternatively, she could tell the rector and/or her husband what, basically, is and is not going on, reasoning that the situation in its salient aspects had now gotten past the reach of confidentiality.

Cases of this sort pose a problem of self-defense to a counselor. The initial premise of confidentiality in such instances can become a hindrance to one's defense; in fact, it can conceivably be a means of unjust oppression against a principled and conscientious person. Surely the best defense in this situation is Anne Jones's own reputation. She is known as the sort of person who does not fall into the kind of situation that the counselee imagines. But Anne Jones also knows that in this "real world" a lot of harm can come simply by gossip and innuendo, and she knows the harm could affect others besides herself. Her deep *feeling* is that a simple duty to keep confidences may be an inadequate response to the situation. She suspects that an underlying premise of good faith, mutual respect, and mental health, which ordinarily buttresses the confidentiality duty, is just not there. Instead, she feels herself a potential victim of someone else's illness. She feels oppressed by injustice, including an unjust demand to keep quiet. She believes that her predicament is not covered any longer by a simple duty of keeping a confidence. (What she might ultimately decide to do, and on what basis, would perhaps depend upon other aspects of her situation. I do not construe this example further, for I am only interested in showing that the need for self-defense may sometimes override the duty of confidentiality.)

There are certain kinds of situations clergy encounter in their roles as pastoral counselors that seem to lie close to, and perhaps beyond, the reach of confidentiality. The duty to keep a confidence is limited in cases where a dangerous person intends, or appears to intend, to commit acts of destruction. It is also limited when the pastor is being asked to cover up a crime, especially an ongoing crime. The alleged "privacy right" is not strongly and unambiguously supported in law, so this cannot always be regarded as a strong incentive to keep confidences in complex situations. Even relationships of special privilege, such as the husband-wife relationship, do not always warrant confidentiality, at least from an ethical point of view, as instances of sexual abuse indicate. Not even the initial promise to keep a confidence is an unyielding guarantee against future disclosure if the evidence suggests that innocent others may be made unduly vulnerable thereby—as in the tale of the child molester.

The duty of clergy especially to keep confidence can be misused either by clergy or by their counselees, as any intrinsically good thing can be misapplied. When clergy are especially faced with situations where malice and/or marked emotional instability are a possibility or when a prudent regard for the destructive power of the inane provokes them to consider (what I have called) self-defense, then they may well believe that the situation has transcended the limits of confidentiality. How these sorts of situations are recognized, appropriately characterized, and responded to is not within the scope of my present purpose. I have intended instead to show that some situations for which the duty to keep a confidence was assumed do not always end up within the limits of that assumption. I quickly and energetically add that cases of the present sort are, mercifully, exceptional and that I agree with all who pronounce that general moral rules are not built upon exceptional cases. Thus, while it remains true that clergy do have, as a rule, a duty to keep confidences, to be slavishly rule-bound could, in certain circumstances, be stupid and destructive. We are called to be human and humanly astute before we are called to be inflexibly legalistic.

6

Professional Ethics and the Law

This chapter will examine the major duties falling upon professionals who have to deal with confidentiality and legally privileged communications. I intend to consider first some of the overall aspects of *role morality*, that is, the basic moral elements at the heart of one's professional role in society. In the next section I will focus specifically on the role of clergy as this relates to issues of legally privileged communications.

Role Morality versus Common Morality

Any professional group exhibits a tendency to curve in upon itself, placing its own interests first, before the interests of others and even before justice. I doubt that I will ever forget a public debate I once had with a seminary professor over the erstwhile clergy and seminarian "IV-D exemption" from conscription into the U.S. armed forces. The debate took place some time during the late 1960s, and I, being opposed to the U.S. effort in Vietnam, was also opposed to that categorical exemption of clergy and seminarians. (The present tale, though not about confidentiality highlights what I regard as a tendency by professional groups to benefit themselves.) My debating opponent was a professor of Old Testament who also was a military chaplain in the navy reserve. He was very much in favor of the U.S. involvement in Vietnam and also in favor of the IV-D clergy exemption. I cannot recall the moral basis of his case in favor of that exemption; I can only remember his extreme annoyance with me for my questioning the special privileges of clergy. I believed that, especially for a class of people accorded some amount of status due to their presumed moral or ethical competence, use of that status as an avoidance didn't make sense. To exclude clergy and seminarians from hard moral choices faced by most others seemed elementally unfair. I believe I was about to elaborate the hypocrisy issue when my opponent's frustrated cries of "Hogwash! Hogwash!" brought things to an abrupt conclusion. The end of the affair suited me well enough, for by then I had precious little support left from the seminary community. (But I still think I'm right. Professionals are accorded status, respect, and various other niceties by morally sensitive people who value the just and virtuous contributions these professionals can, and do, make to others and to society as a whole. For professionals to trade upon their status to gain a self-serving privilege is both a violation of justice and, to be rather pragmatic, an invitation to public ridicule and disrespect.)

The issue that now needs to be identified is the matter of professional role and to what extent an individual engaged in a professional role is affected by role-based morality, rather than the demands ordinarily placed upon him or her as a plain member of society. My debating opponent might have wanted to show that clergy or seminarians have special moral obligations belonging to their role—that is, their membership in the class of ordained people. He might have wanted to demonstrate also that these obligations are of sufficient force to justify the IV-D exemption for clergy. Somewhat consistent with this thinking, my present purpose is to consider role morality as a moral issue in order to focus upon the more narrow and specific concern of role-based confidentiality. Role-based confidentiality, in turn, is most specifically focused in the *legal* context where a confidence between a professional and a nonprofessional, in certain carefully defined situations, is allowed in law as *privileged*. Given the normal duty of ordinary citizens to account for the truth, how strong is the case that certain professionals need not be thus accountable, and upon what is this case based? Let us hold these questions in mind as other role moralities are briefly considered.

Codes of Professional Conduct

Clergy do not generally answer to an explicit code of professional conduct. The various denominations themselves may have canons or guidelines for clergy conduct. The dominant fact is, however, that different religious traditions and denominations are more devoted to affirming their uniqueness (and perhaps their relative autonomies) than to fashioning a comprehensive professional code for all clergy. Certainly the unique differences that separate the Roman Catholic Church or even "high church" Episcopalians, from, say, many Southern Baptist congregations imply major differences in fundamental understandings of clergy and their roles. These differences can imply further differences in normative requirements for clergy conduct. It therefore seems expedient to identify the issue of clergy role morality and privileged communication now, although a more in-depth consideration will be postponed until later in this chapter. Useful insight can first be gained into role morality in general, and the matters of confidentiality and privilege, by looking at some of the thinking that has taken place in other professional areas.

Physicians and Nurses

The American Medical Association (AMA) carefully enjoins physicians to respect the privacy of their patients. However, the AMA "Principles of Medical Ethics," a 1971 statement on confidentiality, also recognizes that such a role-based duty may be overridden. This occurs, for example, when the physician "is required to do so by law or . . . it becomes necessary in order to protect the welfare of the individual or of the society."[1] The physician's duty to keep a confidence is rooted in the very nature of being a doctor, which entails a special role-based relationship with a given patient. The duties to keep a confidence are warranted usually by the AMA "Principles of Medical Ethics" *and* by various state statutes, though some state statutes limit the legal privilege of keeping a confidence to judicial—that is, testimonial —situations only. (Some states allow a physician-patient privilege in criminal but not in civil cases.) But whether a confidence is judicial or extrajudicial, the legal privilege of keeping it can be overridden by the greater needs of others or of society in general. Certain contagious diseases, child abuse, drug abuse, and gunshot wounds are normally subject to mandatory reporting by physicians even when a patient desires to hold the doctor to confidentiality. In some cases close friends or relatives dangerously exposed to the patient's illness have a right to know that they may be infected.[2]

These principles are also true for nurses. The American Nurses Association "Code for Nurses" (1985) places a duty of confidentiality upon nurses, as we might expect. The code wisely adds, "The duty of confidentiality, however, is not absolute when innocent parties are in direct jeopardy."[3] Case studies in nursing ethics cite instances in which an innocent third party may be at risk from a life-threatening illness when the patient has failed to disclose an illness or a genetic disease. Nurses also sometimes become involved in cases where a disturbed patient may be in need of involuntary commitment due to a strong suicidal impulse.

In situations of this sort, the important question is whether the patient's request for confidentiality is being made while he or she is in their "right mind" (this is sometimes an issue of ethics and sometimes of law). A strongly related ethical issue is whether or not a patient can justly involve a nurse in a sort of suicide pact in the sense that confidentiality means that he or she must only stand idly by. Then there are cases of gunshot wounds, reportable venereal disease, child abuse, and the like, concerning which nurses may have the same overriding duties to divulge that physicians have. A nurse, however, is not usually accorded a legal privilege, as a physician may be.

Counselors

Licensed marriage, family, and child counselors are under rules of professional ethics, which hold them to confidentiality; so are others, such as school guidance counselors. These professional ethics codes for counselors are role-morality based. Most states decline to extend a professional legal privilege to such counselors. When it is found in a state statute, the legal privilege is "owned" by the client rather than the counselor, and thus the client may "waive" the privilege—that is, release the counselor to testify.[4] The U.S. Constitution guarantees no ironclad right to privacy for anyone. Thus, no private contract between a counselor or counselee should be based on the assumption that it will always and everywhere protect a confidence against a compulsion to testify.[5] Withal, counselors, like nurses, doctors, and clergy, have socially useful roles to play in U.S. society, and confidentiality is a key part of their role performance. It must be protected appropriately, but so must the public's right to know and especially the right others have to the truth when justice is thwarted by confidentiality used unfairly as a shield.

The Confidentiality Principle in Legal Ethics

The confidentiality principle as developed in the philosophy of law offers a useful approach to understanding the relevant issues of role morality and confidentiality. Two excellent sources— Charles W. Wolfram, *Modern Legal Ethics,*[6] and David Luban, *Lawyers and Justice*[7]—have provided the basis for this discussion.

The principle of confidentiality between an attorney and client is grounded exactly upon the client's need to receive appropriate legal advice. This fact itself points to the unique and socially beneficial professional role of lawyers. The applicable canons, rules, and guidelines for ethical practice by lawyers have been fashioned chiefly by means of American Bar Association (ABA) actions. These are enshrined most notably in the ABA "Code of Professional Responsibility" (the Code), adopted in 1969 and frequently revised since, and the ABA "Model Rules of Professional Conduct" (Model Rules), adopted in 1983 as an alternative to the Code. Regarding confidentiality, the Model Rules limit divulgence to information regarding a future crime involving "imminent death or substantial bodily harm" (MRI.6.b.1). Somewhat para-doxically, this strict rule also allows divulgence by a lawyer when necessary to defend said lawyer against a charge of wrongdoing and when necessary for a lawyer to collect his or her fee (MRI.6.b.2). The ABA Code is more broad on confidentiality than are the Model Rules. It allows exceptions to the confidentiality rule when a court orders the attorney to divulge, when the attorney is aware of a continuing or future fraud or crime being committed, for a lawyer's self-defense against wrongdoing, and to assist a lawyer in collecting a fee (DR 4–101 c 2, 3, and 4).

It is important to note that these two major codes, plus an independent ethics panel unique to California, and other sources (the Kutak Commission report of a special lawyer panel on ethics, the American Trial Lawyer Association, and others), constitute a pool of suggestions, guidelines, exhortations, and proposed standards that any state may draw from in formally adopting professional ethics and in making law. The supreme court of a given state is the body that usually draws from this pool and then enacts particular proposals as normative and legal. It is interesting that, at last count, thirty states had adopted some statement or other governing confidentiality. Half of the states adopted the less stringent confidentiality rule of the Code, and only five states adopted essentially the more narrow and stringent rule of the Model Rules. Nine states chose the relatively flexible rule initially proposed by the Kutak Commission. The evidence shows that prevailing sentiment among the states seems to favor a relatively loose confidentiality rule.[8] This might plausibly be regarded as a preference for getting at the truth even at the cost of weakening the prerogatives of lawyers and their role morality.

Partisanship and Personal Responsibility
The prevailing notion of a lawyer's role is that it entails a principle of partisanship in which the lawyer's zeal to be an advocate is strongly protected. In the case of criminal defense, where the

individual defendant is vulnerable to the massive power of the state, such zeal seems a good thing. We would not want the state to be able to overwhelm individuals easily. Another principle is that of *nonaccountability,* according to which the client's various objectives and means to achieve them are not fundamentally scrutinized and evaluated by the client's lawyer; the lawyer is instead generally presumed to be present to offer a legal service to further the client's chosen end rather than to pass some moral judgment. However, one skeptical philosopher of the law regards all these assumptions as amounting "simply to an institutionalized immunity from the requirements of conscience" for the lawyer.[9] The question being raised by this critique is, Why should lawyers be allowed to escape certain moral accountabilities that are laid normally upon others? Does the professional role of lawyers enable them to evade common morality? And if so, does the fact that lawyers can operate in accordance with the privileges and immunities warranted by criminal defense justify their operating under these assumptions in civil contexts?

A philosophical question that should be answered by anyone filling a professional role is this: Am I, who fill this professional role, still basically a responsible *person?* David Luban writes, "If the true moral agent is 'Me, that poor old ultimate actuality,' whose roles are mere 'lendings,' then it appears that common morality is more truly moral than role morality and should win out in cases where the two conflict."[10] Abdicating personal responsibility, an accountability to common morality, in favor of the morality of one's role requires a decision that the role itself is morally commendable in a rather universal way and that the role itself is inherently moral. But assumptions of this sort are not quickly made by reasonably sophisticated people in today's bureaucratic society. Indeed, the worrisome capacity of large and impersonal bureaucracies these days to grind on and grind people up *anonymously*—that is, with no one personally and visibly responsible—is known not only to readers of Kafka's *Trial* but to everyone who ever received a government assistance check or perhaps a driver's license. The anxiety and inconvenience that attend dealing with anonymous bureaucracies, where no individual seems responsible, can sometimes turn instead into serious harm. This sort of concern is exactly at the center of these remarks by trial judge Miles W. Lord in his splendid remarks to the A.H. Robbins Company senior executives and general counsel in the "Dalkon Shield" case:

Mr. Robins, Fr. Forrest, and Dr. Lunsford: After months of reflection, study, and cogitation—and no small amount of prayer—I have concluded that it is perfectly appropriate to make this statement, which will constitute my plea to you to seek new horizons in corporate consciousness and a new sense of personal responsibility for the activities of those who work under you in the name of the A.H. Robbins Company.

It is not enough to say, "I did not know," "It was not me," "Look elsewhere." Time and again, each of you has used this kind of argument in refusing to acknowledge your responsibility and in pretending to the world that the chief officers and directors of your gigantic multinational corporation have no responsibility for its acts and omissions. . . .

If one poor young man were, without authority or consent, to inflict such damage upon one woman, he would be jailed for a good portion of the rest of his life. Yet your company, without warning to women, invaded their bodies by the millions and caused them injuries by the thousands. And when the time came for these women to make their claims against your company, you attacked their characters. You inquired into their sexual practices and into the identity of their sex partners. You ruined families and reputations and careers in order to intimidate those who would raise their voices against you. You introduced issues that had no relationship to the fact that you had planted in the bodies of these women instruments of death, of mutilation, of disease. . . .[11]

There is a basic ethical problem when professionals allow themselves to evade the claims of common morality by escaping into role morality and its privileges. This problem becomes apparent when we reflect upon the basis for most moral philosophies. Morality in general includes the recognition of someone else's claim upon *me,* rather than my determination to operate *first* from my own presumed needs. Common morality, after all, entails my accepting the entitlements of others; I am here to help *them*—perhaps exactly as a professional—rather than the other way around. My answerability is as a human being to another as a human being. Therefore, *I* prudently bring into play the resources of my profession: I do not manipulate this other, or myself, into a convenient alignment with the stolid requirements of some professional role. "Ultimately we reserve our autonomy from our stations and their duties so that we have the freedom to respond to persons *qua* persons—to obey what one may call the *morality of acknowledgment.*"[12]

From all this, it follows that the primary moral facts are the clients' need for advice and the clients' need for a human response from the individual filling a certain technical role, that is, from another person who happens to be a lawyer. Surely, as between ordinary people, common morality supports the principle of confidentiality. Equally important, too, is that both clients and lawyers have a right to expect predictable and forceful rules buttressing the confidentiality in their relationship. The professional rules for lawyers within any particular state of our nation are there to serve this overall purpose. But the danger, morally speaking, is that injustices may be done if and when lawyers, individually or as a professional class, use the specialized morality of their roles as either a shield for their own self-interest or as a means to subvert truth or justice for others. The aforementioned philosopher, David Luban, believes that confidentiality, as a role-based moral good, tends to make more sense in a criminal defense (against the power of the state) than it does in a civil dispute, where truth and justice frequently take on a different significance and hue, apart from the prospect of state prosecution. Confidentiality must be carefully protected as an aspect of protecting the rights of accused criminals. But even in cases of this sort, there are allowances in all the professional codes.

The Privilege in Legal Ethics

Generally speaking, a *secret* is any communication passing between a client and an attorney that is not intended for disclosure. A *confidential communication* is a secret that the lawyer is duty-bound to conceal from a judicial proceeding. A *privilege* is the decision by a court to regard a confidential communication as indeed inadmissible as legal testimony. The rules a judge may consult in making his or her decision are the same as a lawyer consults when claiming the privilege. To grant the privilege or not, however, is entirely the court's decision.

Charles W. Wolfram's *Modern Legal Ethics* makes the point that society's legitimate need for truth is always to be prized and respected. Therefore, "the predominant judicial view is that the privilege is to be 'strictly construed.' "[13] Wolfram shows some amazement that the attorney privilege is as formidable as it is and speculates that its strength "may be due only to the politically entrenched position of lawyers in courts and legislatures."[14] In other words, lawyers in some degree may have their privilege simply because they are in a position to *get* it. Wolfram goes on to note the "regrettable consequence of overstated claims for the confidentiality principle" in asserting a privilege. He implies that the countervailing disclosure claims ought to be given more consideration "in order to prevent greater harms."[15] For the privilege to be licit, the confidence should have occurred within the context of a client-lawyer communication that is, in fact, legal in nature. Thus, "a lawyer serving as bagman is not serving as a lawyer."[16] Moreover, the particular lawyer must now formally be working on behalf of the client, rather than being a friend, a former advocate for the client, or whatnot.

The privilege actually "belongs" to the client, who can validly waive it: "Once the attorney-client privilege has struggled into existence, it lives a fragile life threatened by forces that can snuff it out. For the most, those forces lie within the power of the client to control. The privilege can be extinguished by the consent of the client. . . ."[17] But there are some circumstances in which an attorney may divulge, even without an explicit waiver. These include the attorney's right to divulge in order to protect himself or herself from allegations of ineffectiveness.[18] Also included is the right to protect the lawyers against the charge of wrongfully settling a case.[19] Accusations of these sorts are regarded as constituting an implied waiver of the privilege for the purpose of the present litigation.

In cases where a crime or fraud is continuing or is contemplated as a future act, an attorney may divulge a confidence even without an implied waiver. *Fraud* in this sort of context is usually taken to mean "all intentional wrongs involving a client acting with bad faith and intending or purposefully oblivious to serious harm to another."[20] It includes the intention by a client to commit perjury, which usually means the commission of a crime (perjury) designed to cover up an earlier crime. ("It would be a perversion of the privilege to extend it so as to protect communications designed to frustrate justice by committing other crimes to conceal past misdeeds.")[21] Similarly, regarding ongoing crimes or frauds in general: "It is indisputable that communications made in furtherance of an ongoing crime are not protected by the attorney-client privilege."[22]

Privilege, Divulgence, and Crimes

It is evident, then, that certain warrants are offered in legal ethics and in the law itself for divulging confidences otherwise coming under the attorney-client privilege. To use only the role morality of a lawyer's privilege simply does not meet instances in which we have deeper, common morality obligations to individuals and to justice in community. The same basic morality that ultimately justifies an appropriate role morality also limits the scope of that morality for the sake of justice itself. The idea is well expressed by David Luban: "Sometimes one clearly ought to break the law. Even if it is illegal to do so, you ought to hotwire my car if that is the only way you can rush a badly injured child to the hospital."[23] Intuitively, we know Luban is correct. We wouldn't want to live in a society in which people dealt with each other strictly by the book. It is less than human to interact with each other that way; more than that, we feel that ordinary decency and moral sensibility are wounded thereby and the overall quality of our lives is diminished.

Let us take a look at some conflicting issues and sensibilities that people have faced in some specific cases. In the first of these, the Lake Pleasant bodies case, one Robert Garrow had been arrested in the Adirondack village of Lake Pleasant on a murder charge.[24] Two Syracuse attorneys, Frank Armani and Francis Belge, defended him. Garrow was suspected of murdering other victims, but he had not yet been charged with these crimes. In their conversations with their client, the attorneys learned that Garrow had indeed killed others. They subsequently discovered the bodies of two of his victims, which they then photographed but about which they felt duty bound to maintain complete silence.

The father of one of these victims flew from Chicago to Syracuse to plead with one of the lawyers for information. The lawyer maintained silence. Subsequently, in Garrow's trial the defendant was put on the witness stand in an attempt to show his insanity. He admitted the two other killings heretofore known only to him and to his lawyers. An immediate uproar took place in the legal community and in the newspapers, with outrage being heaped upon Garrow's lawyers for cleaving so strongly to confidentiality. In subsequent legal proceedings concerning the use of the attorney-client privilege in this case, the New York appeals court upheld the attorneys' privilege not to disclose "insofar as the communications were to advance a client's interests."[25] The appeals court denied the notion of an absolute attorney-client privilege, however, remarking instead that "an attorney must protect his client's interests, but also must observe basic human standards of decency, having due regard to the need that the legal system accord justice to the interests of society and its individual members." The court went on to "emphasize our serious concern" about "an absolute attorney-client privilege" and was careful to limit its vindication of Garrow's lawyers to the narrow specifics of the issues it was asked to adjudicate.[26] Subsequently, the New York State Bar ethics committee vindicated the lawyers, noting that their divulging the information given them in confidence would have violated the ABA "Code of Professional Responsibility," specifically DR4–101(B).[27] We can see here the force and the legitimacy of the privilege in instances involving criminal defense.

Privilege or Divulgence in Civil Litigation

A somewhat different situation is presented, however, in the so-called Spaulding case.[28] Spaulding was seriously injured in a car accident and filed a civil suit to recover damages. The lawyer defending against the suit arranged for a medical examination by a physician of his selection. This physician discovered a severe malady not found by Spaulding's own doctor. A "life-threatening" aortic aneurysm was presumably caused by the defendant but was unknown to Spaulding. Spaulding was already inclined to settle the case for $6,500, and the defense lawyer was aware that if he communicated what he knew about the aneurysm to Spaulding, the terms of the settlement would increase dramatically. (The attorney must also have realized that reporting the aneurysm, so that it might be repaired, could perhaps save Spaulding's life.) Between keeping confidentiality and settling for $6,500 (on the one hand) and disclosing to Spaulding the truth about the aneurysm (on the other hand), the attorney chose the former course. The judge in the case found the attorney's decision "ethically unexceptionable," in the matter of privilege but then, apparently upon learning the truth from the defense lawyer, modified the terms of the settlement to make it more in keeping with the truth and with justice.

In the Spaulding case, the role morality that counseled lawyerly confidentiality was honored by both the attorney and the court. The "real life" circumstances of the case make it difficult, however, for many people to approve the lawyer's silence about what he learned from his own expert; there would seem to be a duty to divulge on grounds of ordinary moral decency. Cases of this sort tend to reinforce David Luban's assertion that there should be a radically different valuation of confidentiality and privilege in the context of civil litigation than there is when the state is menacingly poised in opposition to a criminal defendant.

Lawyers have a different role to play in society than do clergy.

The nature of an attorney-client privilege is different from that of the clergy-penitent privilege. Among other factors, penitents do not have to rely upon clergy to assist them in resisting the formidable power of the state. They do, however, rely upon clergy to assist them in their dealings with God. They also seek help from clergy in dealing with significant others with whom they stand in relationship, with the community in general, and with their own consciences. Sometimes the circumstances that bring a penitent into the office of a clergy person have ramifications of a legal sort. If a clergy person receives a subpoena to testify in court, he or she is obliged to comply with the subpoena. The basic issues, and what may happen to clergy in court, are the concern of the following section.

The Law and Privileged Communications Involving Clergy

Although the specifics governing the compulsion of clergy testimony arise from state statutes regulating the presentation of evidence in court, the larger legal context in which such matters of religion are considered is the First Amendment to the U.S. Constitution. This amendment, which in part was intended to erect a separation between church and state, begins, "Congress shall make no law respecting an establishment of religion or prohibiting the free exercise thereof . . ."[29] Essentially, this establishes two different principles, one in the "establishment" clause and the other in the "free exercise" clause. The two address fundamentally different concepts, but there is substantial enough overlap that court judgments must sometimes favor one of the clauses while antagonizing the other. The frequency and recognizability of this has led to a familiar expression in legal discourse; this is of the "natural antagonism" between the two clauses. Courts have consistently sought to strike a neutral balance between the two clauses but not always successfully.

The First Amendment was initially intended to limit the power of the federal government by prohibiting Congress from passing laws that offended its enumerated principles. It was later interpreted by the Supreme Court to apply to the states, based upon the Fourteenth Amendment's due process clause.[30] The prohibition now extends to state legislative action.[31] It applies to judicial action as well.[32] State courts, therefore, are guided ultimately by state laws formulated within the framework of the federal Constitution.

The First Amendment establishment clause prohibits government sponsorship of religion by aid or establishment. Courts have judged the constitutionality of laws or state actions under the clause using a three-part test: The law's purpose must be secular; its primary effect must neither advance nor prohibit religion; and it must not draw the government into an "excessive entanglement" with religion.[33] This last standard is somewhat vague, and therefore it is interpreted in particular instances with the help of another three-part test: What is the nature and purpose of the religious institution likely to be helped? What sort of aid is being proposed? What is the likely involvement of government and religious authorities with each other?[34] As an example, the California Supreme Court has held that a state constitution provision that requires the state to make reasonable accommodation for an employee to practice the tenets of his or her religion does not run afoul of the establishment clause although, interestingly, the U.S. Supreme Court has not passed on the issue.[35]

The other clause of the First Amendment, the "free exercise" clause, expressly forbids government interference in any religious beliefs. Actions based upon those beliefs, however, are under certain circumstances open to state intervention—even though a religious view might regard the sundering of beliefs from action a dubious business. Still, acts and secular activities of religious organizations may be regulated when the state interprets its own interest as more important than the countervailing interest of a religious entity to be free from such regulation. In cases of conflict, the courts consider the degree to which the free exercise of a religion would be burdened in contrast to the degree to which the regulation of religious acts should be undertaken by the state. Thus, the Supreme Court ruled that there was no violation of the free exercise clause in a federal law requiring the Amish to violate the tenets of their faith by participating in the Social Security system.[36] While ordinarily the burden of proving a violation of such statutes lies with the prosecution, the defendant has the burden of proof as to affirmative defenses. Therefore, if the defense is based on unconstitutionality under the First Amendment, a church could be required to show that the undesired state regulation struck significantly at the belief-based practices of religion—that is, that it burdened religion unduly.

In another area, the courts have intervened in religious activity, despite strong attempts to keep the government neutral with respect to religion under the free exercise clause. This involves the practical implications of religious beliefs, as, for example, when pursuit of religious beliefs might compromise the health and safety of others. There is the familiar instance of civil courts transferring to the state the custody of children who need blood transfusions when their Jehovah Witness parents refuse to consent to treatment on religious grounds. This is done to enable the children to sustain their health and viability even though the parents' religious beliefs regard blood transfusions as prohibited by God. Courts have repeatedly held that, although parents may have the right to believe what they wish, they do not have the right to expose their children to the risk of death as a result of their beliefs.

Still another area in which government has limited what some regard as the free exercise of religion has to do with the rules of evidence regarding testimony by clergy. Courts have compelled clergy to testify in many cases. When do clergy possess a privilege not to testify? Who decides? On what basis?

Clergy Privilege

The development of the clergy-communicant privilege is clearly and comprehensively traced by Jacob M. Yellin in an article entitled "The History and Current Status of the Clergy-Penitent Privilege"[37] He notes that English common law, which forms the basis for much of the law in the United States, seemed to provide privilege for clergy up until the time of the Protestant Reformation. Thereafter, the privilege ceased to exist in England. Yellin cites numerous cases in post-Reformation England where the privilege was simply denied. In England today, even if a minister claims to possess confidential information, he or she may not claim a privilege in law: "Confessions made to a minister of religion under the seal of secrecy are not privileged from disclosure," according to *II Halsbury's Laws of England*.[38]

In the United States, where there is some degree of church and state separation, the case history reveals instances in which the courts, in enforcing state statutes, have specifically allowed the privilege to be asserted and honored. But in a significant number of cases a privilege was not conferred. A primary policy reason for conferring privilege is that doing so is socially useful, as some people are thereby better able to receive the healing ministrations and/or spiritual counsel of the church. Other reasons include the court's recognition that some clergy will not divulge confidences under any circumstances and that trying to force disclosures in such instances would not meet with community approbation.

The court also recognizes that the First Amendment free exercise clause leaves room for the privilege to be conferred. (But this last reason is not, according to Yellin, accorded "great weight by legal theoreticians.")[39]

While virtually all American states recognize some sort of clergy-communicant privilege, there is substantial variation as to specifics. This is primarily because, in adjudicating crimes and civil disputes, courts have a fundamental interest in ascertaining truth. The chief means to this end is to compel competent, material, and relevant testimony, limiting as much as possible the exceptions to such compulsion. Unprivileged refusal to testify is punishable by fine or imprisonment as contempt of court; untruthful testimony (perjury) is a felony. It is not surprising that privileges against testifying are allowed only with reservation and then only when allowing them is amply justified by public policy considerations. That is, in law these exceptions to the general rule of compelling testimony do not in any sense proceed from a presumed right that inheres in confidentiality itself.

The evidentiary statutes that give life to testimonial privileges derive from state statutes that, as we have seen, must not run afoul of the federal Constitution. They are generally written narrowly and applied conservatively. The California statutory scheme is typical in some aspects and more liberal in others. In California, both penitents and clergy have the privilege to refuse to disclose a *penitential communication.* A penitential communication is defined more liberally in California than in most states as "a communication made in confidence, in the presence of no third person so far as the penitent is aware, to a clergyman who, in the course of the discipline or practice of his church, denomination or organization, has a duty to keep such communications secret."[40] In addition, a penitent, whether he or she is a party in a certain case, may refuse to disclose and can prevent others from disclosing his or her penitential communication. In California, the clergy person also has the privilege to refuse to disclose, even if the penitent does not claim it, as the law will not compel clergy to violate the tenets of their church that require them to maintain secrecy of confidential statements.[41] The clergy are not duty bound to claim the privilege, however. Thus in California, if the penitent is dead, incompetent, absent, or fails to claim his privilege, the clergy person might elect to testify.[42]

More typically, however, the state statutes are "subject to strict construction and the coverage confined to verbal communications which are both confidential and penitential, and made to persons acting in the capacity of clergyman or spiritual advisors, in the course of the discipline enjoined by the particular denomination."[43] The "confidential and penitential" phrase is crucial. Thus, William H. Tiemann and John C. Bush, in *The Right to Silence: Privileged Clergy Communication and the Law,* report the order by a Pennsylvania court compelling the testimony of a Roman Catholic priest concerning a communication made to him "in the course of the priest's duties" but not in confidence.[44] Concerning the "capacity" question, attorney Richard R. Hammar, writing in *Pastor, Church and Law,* asserts, "Most state laws require that the communication be made to a clergyman acting in the professional capacity as a spiritual advisor"—rather than, say, the pastor's capacity as a church administrator.[45] In a 1965 California case, for instance, a rabbi was left unprotected by the then-existing clergy privilege statute. Shortly before the California statute was expanded, the court ruled that, though the rabbi was a party to a confidence, this was in his role as a marriage counselor, deemed an administrative capacity, rather than in his role as a rabbi.[46] Presumably the court inferred that the rabbi's discipline did not require secrecy of such confidences. The court's decision on whether to confer the privilege in a given case may be based on whether the communication was made to a priest while he or she was in the "professional character." This normally means that the priest is at the moment functioning in a mode expressly anticipated as sacerdotal at his or her ordination—say, as a spiritual counselor rather than as an accidental witness to a crime. "It is only confidential communications made to a clergyman in his spiritual capacity which the law endeavors to protect."[47]

Another aspect of the privilege is that in many states it may be conferred more readily in instances where the clergy person claiming it does so on the basis of the "discipline enjoined" upon him or her explicitly by the religious denomination. This is, in fact, a requirement in some statutory schemes such as California's (mentioned above). In examining whether the clergy person's discipline enjoins silence, the court will look to the tenets of the clergy person's order to determine if it prohibits revealing the information under consideration. If not, there is no protection. Yellin notes the Roman Catholic position with its most rigid and explicitly enjoined discipline prohibiting priests from divulging information obtained in the confessional "even in order to prevent harm to third persons." Interestingly, he adds that in the Roman Catholic tradition the identical information as that obtained in a confession would not be privileged if communicated outside the confessional, even if that communication were made with the expectation of professional secrecy.

Another lawyer and expert in church/state relations, Leo Pfeffer, announced simply, "There is no constitutional right to confession," though the various state statutes specifying the precise circumstances within which a clergy-communicant privilege can be invoked are valid ultimately under the Constitution's free exercise clause. Pfeffer goes on to cite two instances for which confidentiality should not be allowed as privileged: one in which a priest learns "about an evil that is not yet complete and can be stopped" and one in which an injustice will otherwise occur—as when, for example, a priest knew from a confession that a condemned person was truly innocent. "Free exercise of religion is subordinate to justice," said the attorney.[48]

In general, then, the particularities of different cases and their exigent requirements for testimony largely frame the courts' decisions concerning the admissibility and compulsion of testimony. What will be regarded as privileged, and what will not, will be determined on a case-by-case basis as the court, in all likelihood, narrowly applies an already narrowly constructed state statute. Clergy who find themselves faced with the prospect of involvement in litigation should be aware that laws, and the application of laws to particular cases, are an uncertain business. The prudent course of action is always to seek competent legal counsel and appropriate support from local and regional church authorities.

7

Managing Yourself and Parish under the Impact of Litigation

How one loves God, serves the people to whom one ministers, and attends appropriately to the needs of self and immediate family all at the same time is an enduring mystery. Clergy usually agree that all these things must be done, even when we are not sure how it is possible. The record of each clergy person's negotiation of these competing claims is the story of each one's unique life. There is no formula for success in responding to the future. We are given the pattern of Christ's life, teaching, affirming and forgiving love; all this is a guide and a help. But each person must go forward in his or her own path, responding uniquely to emerging events and discovering in the pattern of response who each is coming to be. We can be certain of our chief duty to love and serve God; sorting out the penultimate duties, the conflicting duties, is sometimes not a simple matter.

When a truly extraordinary event takes place, the overall context of our personal and professional life can be contorted. The recognizable patterns and configurations of our lives are twisted; what was formerly the natural feel of things, the intuitively known way of acting, changes. We have to think about things we earlier had the luxury of not having to think about. Litigation, public scrutiny, allegations or suspicions of wrong-doing all combine to create an entirely new situation. The more worrisome implications of this stem from pressures that can be associated with a siege mentality: Instead of an earlier sense of approbation, there is now a feeling of uncertainty; when before there seemed to be forward momentum in one's ministry, there is now a thought to covering bases and offering explanations. The whole matter of loving God and choosing between the different duties we have is changed because the context of our overall ministry—and our personal life—becomes distorted.

A symptom of overall contextual distortion may well be the feeling one has that he or she is placed now in an adversarial role. There can even be a sense in which being an adversary (within

the distortion) seems to be an aspect of a positive duty to love—
to love and serve the parish presently under threat. One does not
come easily to an equation of "adversary" with "duty to love,"
for the context in which we prefer to operate makes this association seem odd. It is normally easier for us to imagine an adversarial
role as incompatible with a duty to love. But an attack upon the
community can change the overall structure of things. Loving the
community can come to mean being adversarial to the attack
upon it.

We experienced such a thing in the parish I serve, and what
was learned from it is offered now, along with other insights that
have been gleaned over several years of parish ministry, as a
possible help to others. The great bulk of this chapter will be made
more clear and useful by my presenting here, verbatim, the
"Facts" portion of a June 9, 1988, California appeals court
opinion regarding a case in which we were involved. I have
changed the "Facts" section of that opinion only to the extent
of using initials instead of names for all others than myself. (The
appeals court unanimously upheld the trial court that heard the
case originally. The defendant then appealed to the California
Supreme Court, which refused to review the case, leaving both
the verdict and sentence in place.) The case is 203 Cal App. 3d
1358 (1988).

We recite the factual background against which the claim of statutory
privilege is presented. (The facts underlying the embezzlement counts
are essentially undisputed.) (During her testimony, defendant essentially
admitted misappropriation of funds from the several accounts which
were entrusted to her management. It appears that by the time of trial,
she had made substantial—if not full—restitution of the defalcations.)
Around 8:30 p.m. on Sunday, August 5, 1984, defendant S.
telephoned Father William Rankin, the rector of St. Stephen's Episcopal
Church in Belvedere, and said she urgently needed to talk to him about
"a problem." Father Rankin, who was scheduled to leave early the
next morning to attend a week-long meeting in Oklahoma, asked
defendant, a church member, if her problem could wait until he
returned. After defendant related she had already talked to Father G.,
another priest affiliated with St. Stephen's, who told her it was
imperative to see Father Rankin immediately, they arranged to meet
that evening at Father Rankin's office. At the meeting, defendant first
declared she had done something almost "as bad as murder." She then
requested that their conversation be confidential; Father Rankin agreed.
Defendant proceeded to tell Father Rankin that she needed his help
in stopping payment on certain checks drawn against the account of
St. Stephen's Guild, of which she served as treasurer. (In fact, the Guild
account was practically depleted due to her embezzlement of nearly

$30,000 over a period of many months.) Defendant told him she had arranged to borrow money to cover her misappropriation but needed his help because the loan proceeds would not be available in time to prevent the checks authorized for issuance to various charities from being dishonored.

Because he was leaving the following day, Father Rankin believed he would be unable to provide a solution and eventually suggested two alternatives to defendant: he could keep her revelation in confidence as agreed, or he could talk to the church wardens on her behalf seeking their help in solving the problem. As the lay leaders of the church, the wardens were responsible for its financial affairs. Defendant consented to the latter option. Father Rankin repeated the question whether that was the course of action defendant wanted to pursue, and she assured him it was. However, defendant testified that she felt she had no choice but to agree. (During that same conversation, defendant also revealed that she had taken funds from the accounts of several doctors for whom she managed property. Those defalcations are the basis of three of the charged counts consolidated for trial.)

Later that evening, Father Rankin called D.K., the senior warden, and informed him of defendant's visit and the two alternatives he presented. K. agreed to handle the problem in Father Rankin's absence. Father Rankin also called S.O., the junior warden, and asked her to attempt retrieval of the (worthless) checks before they were presented for payment; her efforts ultimately proved successful.

During the week of his absence, Father Rankin and the two wardens remained in frequent contact with defendant, but no resolution was reached. K. testified that defendant told him she had taken some $27,000, which could not be discovered in an audit. (According to O. defendant told her she had burned the incriminating checks.) (Defendant testified that her purpose in seeking Father Rankin's help was to prevent the imminent public disclosure of insufficient funds in the Guild's bank account. She stated her intention was to cover up her misdeeds once she had replenished the depleted account with funds from the materialized loan.)

K. thereafter scheduled a meeting of the 15-member vestry for Saturday, August 11. Before the meeting, defendant showed Father Rankin a telegram from a loan agency indicating her loan had been approved. Upon the request of the vestry, defendant delivered to them pertinent records and documents with the explanation that she had destroyed some of the checks. Acting upon the advice of the controller of the diocese, the vestry decided the missing funds had to be reported to the police because their fidelity bond was otherwise at risk. Soon thereafter, K. and other church members reported the incident to the local police resulting in the issuance of a search warrant. Various bank records, ledgers and canceled checks seized during the authorized search of defendant's house were admitted in evidence at trial.

At the conclusion of the evidentiary stage of trial, the court determined that the clergy-penitent privilege did not apply and, in any event, was limited to testimonial as opposed to extrajudicial statements. The court then found defendant guilty as charged, including an enhancement pursuant to Penal Code section 12022.6, subdivision (a). Thereafter, sentence was suspended and defendant placed on formal probation subject to certain conditions including four months in jail.

The allusion in the final paragraph above to the clergy-penitent privilege is the key to the overall situation, legally speaking. The trial transcript shows that the defendant's strategy was to attempt to persuade the court that her request of me to conceal her crimes against the church amounted to a confession that should have been kept forever "sealed." She admitted in testimony that she had asked me to contact the church wardens. Her attorney argued, however, that I was not free to comply with her request, since the 1979 prayer book rubric regarding the "Reconciliation of a Penitent" holds that confessions are forever sealed, under all circumstances. The defendant's position was that since all the evidence against her in court had come to light in a direct succession following our one conversation, that evidence should be suppressed; it had come about in a way that infringed her right, she claimed, to a sealed conversation. The court found that there had been no confession of the sort that warrants coverage by the priest-penitent privilege. Nor had we been using the prayer book ceremony regarding the "Reconciliation of a Penitent" where the rubric concerning the seal applies.

Much could be quoted from both the preliminary hearing transcript (no. 08404240) and the trial transcript itself to demonstrate the above analysis. The essence of the defendant's strategy can perhaps be conveyed most conveniently by my quoting directly from the trial transcript (AO–32616, vol. 3, pp. 339ff.). Here I use only initials where appropriate, as before. At the end of the trial the defendant's attorney questioned the court's finding that the conversation between the defendant and me was not privileged: "Now, the people's (prosecution's) whole case is built on the information that went from Father Rankin to D.K., ultimately from D.K. to the police, who then used the information to get a search warrant to get the records and that's how they got into the case." At this point the judge began to respond, "I accept that, but what difference does it make? . . . ." The defense attorney replied, "The statutory privilege, to have any meaning, would have to mean that you could object to the introduction of—based on the privilege—introduction of evidence, be it testimonial records or what not, because it's almost all gained because of the violation of the privilege." The judge replied,

". . . I don't know of any rule of law that suggests that a search warrant is invalid because the information upon which a search warrant is based stops you from some privileged conversation. . . ." Eventually the defense lawyer remarked, "Of course, our theory is—we haven't found cases in California to support that or really anywhere in the sections. The fact that but for what Father Rankin did this whole case would collapse. D.K. wouldn't have had the information that he took to the Belvedere Police Department." The defendant's hope seemed to be to have evidence suppressed because of some violation of a privileged communication. The judge, however, persisted in his judgment that there was no privileged communication between the defendant and me. He found the defendant guilty and scheduled a date for sentencing.

Then came a civil lawsuit. Exactly one year after the conversation between the defendant and me—and some months after her criminal convictions—the defendant became plaintiff. I, the bishop, various diocesan officials, my vestry, and various parishioners were named as defendants in a $5 million lawsuit. The publicity attending the civil suit was considerable. The plaintiff's lawyer appeared on local radio and television talk shows. The charges of emotional distress, fraud, invasion of privacy, negligence, breach of fiduciary duty, and conspiracy were widely reported. I have clippings from over thirty-five newspapers, including the *London Daily Telegraph,* the *Johannesburg Star,* and the *Jerusalem Post.* (I never thought I'd be mentioned in *Playboy* magazine, but behold, there I was!) ABC's "20/20" did a segment on the case, and National Public Radio got into it, too. It appeared in religious publications of various sorts.

Many of the headlines in various papers and sometimes the gist of the printed story itself were arresting and dramatic: An unfortunate woman makes a sacramental confession to her priest, who immediately calls the police and has her arrested. The lawsuit (no. 844020) contained many stock legal terms that are frequently used in such cases. One example is where the plaintiff alleges the following as cause of action: "plaintiff made a sacramental confession . . . plaintiff further requested (confidentiality); Rankin . . . released . . . confidential information . . . causing plaintiff to be criminally prosecuted." There follows a lengthy recitation of resulting emotional distress to plaintiff; plaintiff was hurt by "willful, fraudulent, malicious" actions, by me and other church people. We operated presumably with "conscious disregard of plaintiff's rights, with the intent to vex, annoy, harass and injure plaintiff." The allegations went on: There were, presumably, secret intentions not to honor the "sacramental nature of confessions," "negligent representations"; there was "intent to defraud," "invasion of privacy," "negligence," "breach of fiduciary duty," and, finally, "conspiracy."

It is perhaps apparent that the key issue in the criminal trial—namely, the issue of an alleged violation of the seal of confession—was at the heart of the civil lawsuit as well. Following the criminal convictions, the California appeals court upheld the trial court in finding that "the questioned statement was not a penitential communication within legal contemplation" and that "no privilege attached" to it. Referring to a situation in which a bona fide confession might indeed take place, where the seal of confession would be in effect, the court said, "Where such determination is supported by substantial, credible evidence, as shown, we are duty bound to uphold it" (203 Cal App 3d 1358 [1988]). The end of the criminal appeal finally came in the summer of 1989, when the United States Supreme Court refused to review the case. Soon after that, the civil lawsuit was dismissed and the entire process, which had begun nearly five years earlier, was concluded.

As I said earlier, I believe it is useful to offer others the things I have learned about how to handle the sometimes bizarre dynamics of litigation—the intrapsychic and intraparish dynamics. Much of what follows, however, is *not* related to this case; rather, it is the consequence of twenty-three years' general experience in the ordained ministry.

Litigation presents unique challenges to the rector of a parish. I am fortunate to be serving a parish whose staff, lay people, and lay leadership are extraordinarily wise. They are also agreeably supportive of one another and of me. Especially during the moments of greatest outrage for me, when newspapers, radio, and television accounts were presenting only the woman's side of this story, I was unduly vulnerable to anger and disgust. I have been terribly lucky and blessed in the bargain to have had the support of wonderful people. They helped me respond to the uproar and confusion in ways that were affirmative and protective of me, the parish as a whole, my family, and the entire church. Many of the ideas set forth below must be credited to them, in considerable degree. I hope that what we all learned will be helpful to others who find themselves, or their parish, involved in criminal litigation or in civil lawsuits or scrutinized by possibly opportunistic media people.

The Ethos of Parish Administration

The Principle of Openness

A wise friend told me many years ago that the best way—perhaps the only healthy way—to be a sound institutional leader is to say and do all things pertaining to management in an atmosphere of radical openness. Everything should be done as if under the noonday sun, he said; otherwise, you and those around you will eventually end up in *some* kind of trouble. Certainly he was not referring to confidential communications; rather, he was referring to the general climate of an institution, the spirit of a place. He was talking about a quality of conducting organizational leadership. In my mind the basic openness of which he spoke is quite opposed to such unhealthy and covert practices as the mystification of the laity by unctious clergy; even the tacit encouragement of "in-groups"; personality cults around the clergy; undue control by those granted more information; and so forth. I don't think that, within the context of parish administration, allowing or fostering mystification in general or secrecy in particular is either practical or in the spirit of Jesus. Indeed, having many secrets typically implies a *need* to be secretive on someone's part, and this tendency to be secretive has the inevitable consequence of generating mistrust; mistrust is not the stuff of which Christian community is either built or sustained.

In her new book, *A Strategy for Peace,* Sissela Bok salutes the ability of Gandhi to build and maintain an organization of the finest moral integrity.[1] Nonviolence was, of course, a salient quality of Gandhi's organizations. But another was Gandhi's militant "concern for truthfulness and truth": There was a profound openness in his dealings with others. Bok writes, "Finally, Gandhi rejected secrecy in his dealings with supporters as with those who opposed him. He regularly sent his policy statements and plans to those who might oppose him, to give them an opportunity to respond in the search for a just solution." After tracing the pragmatic reasons for Gandhi's openness, Bok concludes with this point, whose relevance to any organization, including a parish, is by no means remote: "Secrecy in political work, moreover, would have exposed him to government spies and agents provocateurs, with all the smears and scandal they can generate."[2]

Again, stressing simply the pragmatic advantages of openness in organizations, Bok writes this of the Solidarity movement in Poland: "But the movement is far more accessible both to Poles and to foreign media and sympathizers than secret resistance groups under repressive regimes usually are. . . . Solidarity's openness and broad media contacts have helped it to gain widespread international support."[3] Surely there is much that is dissimilar between the dynamics of a parish, an Indian freedom movement, and the Polish Solidarity movement of today. But what they have in common is a need for moral integrity and for the goodwill and voluntary support of their members. Without these they could hardly be what they claim to be. With them, there is an approbation and admiration among people of en-lightened moral sensibilities, and this is what gives them their dignity, value, integrity, power, credibility, and effectiveness.

A high degree of openness is required of the leaders of institutions and organizations who lay special claim to a high degree of moral credibility. Pastor-parishioner relationships illustrate that point plainly. Only in a climate of openness and trust (of which openness is both cause and effect) may the deepest confidences be exchanged in pastoral counseling. This is because parishioners usually intuit whether the pastoral, as well as the overall parish, ambience is morally healthy and honorable. If they are able to intuit that it is, they will be trusting of the clergy. The clergy, for their part, will honor that trust because they have shown themselves to be honorable in their leadership. Openness in administration, the nourishment of trust, and the integrity of confidence-keeping within the pastoral counseling setting are all aspects of the pervasive atmosphere of parish integrity. These qualities mutually reinforce each other.

Primum non Nocere

For clergy who have knowledge of other clergy or parishes facing litigation, one of the most useful of all ethical maxims comes from the ancient Hippocratic Oath. This is a professional code originating before the time of Jesus and still administered to people about to enter medical practice: *Primum non nocere,* first do not harm. There are seemingly countless situations of formidable complexity that require a decision from a priest. Even when one does not know the best option to choose, one can frequently rule out choices likely to cause harm. I apply this principle to the particular business of collegiality among clergy when one of us is faced with the multiple problems and confusions of litigation, adverse publicity, and the impact these can have on our parish, our family, and ourselves.

In the earliest days of the controversy affecting my parish, the media printed the first stories of the arrest of a parishioner for embezzlement and grand theft. I felt that to say anything to the press would be both undignified and unnecessarily hurtful to the parish and to the person under arrest. But this meant that I needed to find a way to convey accurate information, at least minimally, to those whose confusion, based on their having heard only one side of the story, posed some threat to the parish community. (There were initially a few parishioners who misunderstood the facts, believing erroneously that our parish leadership had acted improperly and hurtfully toward the accused embezzler.) During this time, while the leadership jointly devised a clear and appropriate means to disseminate accurate information, the parish stood to be hurt. The unpredictable effects of controversy, misinformation, and confusion were a source of worry in this earliest stage in the process.

Collegiality among clergy is not clubbish and surely not the same thing as a blood oath among scoundrels to protect one another at all costs. But by the same token, when one clergy person is having to deal with this sort of situation, surely his or her colleagues as a general rule ought to abide by the principle of *primum non nocere*. That is to say, if the Reverend Joe Jones or the Reverend Jane Doe has a daunting controversy surrounding him or her, collegiality means at a minimum that I, being a priest, will not intrude upon that situation or otherwise appropriate it for my own purposes. Let me illustrate this point autobiographically.

During this particularly fragile period of time, a clergy person now living a considerable distance away, having heard only a highly biased and self-serving account of our difficulty, made numerous phone calls to parishioners to align them against the rector and vestry. Another clergy person chose to speak twice from his pulpit about our difficulties during the same period of time—the second sermon coming after I asked him to cease this hurtful practice and he promised that he would. Still another clergy person (who later admitted having no personal or direct knowledge of the case at hand) appeared as an expert witness in church law in the criminal trial. His testimony was part of (an ultimately unsuccessful) scheme designed to discredit a fellow priest, and it was, incidentally, contrary to the testimony of a bishop. Each of these clergy people may have thought he or she was doing the right thing. The information of each, however, was badly biased, incomplete, or just plain wrong. But even more to my present purpose, I wonder on what basis each of them, being so far removed from the facts and the people of the case, formulated so definitive and harsh a judgment against us. I believe a certain kindness, or at least prudence, would counsel due care among clergy in showing appropriate professional regard for their colleagues—even when their positions are quite opposed.

Somewhat more on the salubrious side, during our time of difficulty our church received an enormous outpouring of support, by mail and telephone, from priests and bishops from all across the church. It was a wonderful thing. Not surprisingly, now that I reflect upon it, I also heard from a number of physicians, especially when publicity attended the filing of the civil suit. I discovered what physicians have long experienced —the bizarre feelings you get when you are targeted by a lawsuit. I don't mean to say, incidentally, that all suits against physicians, or clergy, are groundless. But when one comes your way, you get an amazing range of feelings! The main point, however, is that clergy can be appropriately supportive of one another by first doing no harm and by not rushing to judgment from long distances.

The Principle of Discernment

A clergy person ought to possess, and be able to nourish, a certain quality of discernment, an ability to discriminate between one kind of situation and another. We have to be able to characterize different problems appropriately so that we can then dispose ourselves accordingly. For example, the range of possible solutions to an administrative problem will be different, of course, from the range of other solutions to a pastoral problem. Long before the adolescent delinquent in "West Side Story" announced, "I'm depraved on account of I'm deprived," pastoral solutions have opportunistically been sought for problems that are not *essentially* pastoral.

Clergy are frequently approached by people presenting complex problems who seek only a "pastoral" response to them. Groups such as Alcoholics Anonymous recognize that a response frequently passing for pastoral, let's say supportive listening, can be by itself destructive. After all, to be "supportive" or "nurturing" *only* may well make you part of the problem rather than part of its solution. Perhaps other responses are called for instead. Being able validly to recognize a problem as having administrative or managerial aspects is crucial. Even more crucial is the ability to recognize pastoral or administrative problems with legal implications.

I have been privileged to serve a splendid parish in a large urban area. Thus, I have long been aware of the unique difficulties that clergy doing urban "street ministry" can encounter. Without making sweeping generalizations concerning all homeless people, I recall what is currently accepted by many: There is a relatively high incidence of emotionally disturbed people in the homeless population. Clergy who undertake heroic, specialized ministries among folks who are called "the homeless mentally ill" (I regret the phrase) sometimes find themselves in difficult situations as a consequence.[4] Clergy working in this sort of context learn to be careful. They have discovered that an important part of discernment also entails exercising due care in their dealings with a troubled person. If you feel vaguely uneasy or mistrustful of someone, there may be a valid reason for that feeling. I believe those feelings should be respected and explored for their possible meanings. Some people who end up causing much trouble, grief, or heartache to individuals and institutions could have been identified as troubled and capable of behaving destructively. Clergy doing street ministries are in especially difficult spots in cases like this because people of every possible sort seek them out, correctly perceiving clergy to be sympathetic. The clergy themselves tend to be, and are in some respects obliged to be, accepting of all sorts and conditions of people. To be accepting, however, is not the same thing as being mindless. We are not asked, nor are we obliged, to risk or sacrifice our personal integrity or the parish's overall security every time we face a demand from an individual. Indeed, clergy surely have some obligation to protect themselves and their parishes.

No physician, so far as I am aware, is morally bound in the normal course of things to accept any or all patients. When one becomes a professional, one does not on that account give up one's autonomy. This applies to clergy. Clergy are frequently *assumed* and sometimes *expected* to minister to *anybody*. But a priest who complies with such an expectation uncritically will get into difficulty sooner or later. We do the best we can with whoever comes our way, but we are the stewards of our own lives and the institutions we serve, too. Certainly we take people, problems, confidences, and confessions with utmost seriousness. Being personally responsible means being able to respond by making judicious and discriminating decisions. And yet, and yet . . . ! Although I am keenly aware of the risks of putting it this starkly, I nonetheless state what we all know or should know: One of the unfortunate but necessary decisions clergy sometimes have to make is to treat troubled people in special ways, by trying to drastically limit the damage they can cause others. The *basis* for decisions of this sort should not be our own arbitrariness or our own autonomy. Rather, the basis should be a sincere respect for our limitations as paraprofessionals in counseling and for the entire community we pastor. We are on more solid ground when we recognize our limitations and refer complex situations to competent others. Their training and experience equips them to deal appropriately with people we cannot adequately help.

Counseling Precautions

When approaching any counseling situation, one should be aware of some general guidelines. In light of the possibility of litigation, any parish priest counseling another person should avoid charging a fee for such counseling or even suggesting a donation to the church, lest in a court's mind pastoral counseling becomes confused with professional counseling. A different set of standards may apply to professional counseling, and First Amendment immunities and prerogatives of clergy may then not apply. Clergy counseling is normally *gratis*, and it is not exactly the same thing as professional counseling.

Any church institution offering licensed, professional clergy counseling should require these counselors to carry their own professional liability insurance. Further, any clergy finding themselves dealing with "counselees who show evidence of substance, physical, mental or sexual abuse or who display signs of poor mental health" should make a clear referral to competent others.[6] When this is done, it is crucial that clergy have the counselee sign a statement certifying that such a referral occurred.

As noted earlier, a conversation occurring in confidence, which subsequently takes a turn in the direction of divulgence, requires a free, informed mutual consent to divulge. Such free and informed consent is a valid waiver of confidentiality, and the circumstances may suggest that such a waiver be in written form, signed and dated by the counselee. Clearly the circumstances may not warrant this degree of caution; one does not want to be either defensive or insulting to a parishioner. If there is some doubt about the overall integrity of the counselor-counselee relationship, however, it is wise to obtain a written waiver.

Managing the Parish During a Time of Litigation

Record Keeping

If you find yourself in a situation from which litigation is likely to result, you will probably know it immediately. Someone, for example, who is faced with the imminent discovery of a crime he or she has committed and who asks you to cover up what has been done is in all likelihood going to be caught up in the justice system. You may be, too. To pose another example, anyone who comes to you for any reason and goes away enraged is a possible plaintiff against you in a civil lawsuit. This is because one of the motives for suing someone is to get revenge. Another motive for lawsuits—unquestionably the most commonly encountered—is plain old greed. Most people sue other people for money. In many cases, although you may feel targeted, there is truly nothing personal about things from the plaintiff's point of view. The plaintiff isn't out for you so much as for your money!

In any event, given your commonsense ability to recognize trouble when you see it and given that people sue for vengeance or (more likely) money, you should keep a careful record of precisely what did and didn't happen in any situation that holds a high potential for legal involvement. You should also, of course, conduct yourself with utmost kindness, clarity, and probity in that situation, since you may have to explain yourself to a court later. Moreover, in keeping written records, be aware that these may be subpoenaed and could be entered into evidence in any legal proceeding. Written records may have to be explained or defended in court, and your advance awareness of this is crucial. The bottom line is that you are on the most solid ground if you have been careful, competent, respectful, law-abiding, and well intentioned in every situation, though being well intentioned *alone* will not necessarily protect you in court. A clergy person's best defense is to have approached a troubled and complex situation with all-around integrity and competence.

111

Notification of Others

If you receive reliable information that litigation is likely to affect you or the parish, or that one of your parishioner's legal entanglements may have implications for you or the parish, you should immediately notify your judicatory executive (in my case, the bishop) and the appropriate judicatory legal counsel (in my case, the diocesan chancellor). These officials are entitled to know about any trouble on your horizon, since they are at least remotely implicated in actions that affect you professionally or affect your parish. They also can be of enormous help. (Of course, if you are bound by confidentiality concerning any aspect of pending litigation, you will be limited in what you can say to anyone!)

Normally the bishop should not be drawn into litigation if that can be avoided, and an important duty of the chancellor is to prevent such a thing from happening. Indeed, the overall credibility of the church is placed in jeopardy whenever any of its officials are brought into the justice system for any reason— not least because of their vulnerability to media people whose own professional ethics, sense of fairness, or respect for the truth are entirely unknown.

The personal support of the bishop and the legal resources of the judicatory through the chancellor can be of considerable help. One should be aware, of course, that neither the bishop nor chancellor is free to support misconduct or incompetence on your part, either within the context of litigation or generally. They are bound first and foremost by the truth, as you are. (The worst case scenario would be that you have committed an offense of some sort that is being scrutinized in court; the bishop cannot do much for you in such situations, and you would be naive to expect to be rescued at this juncture.)

Exercising Caution

Assuming that you now know of litigation pending that will affect you or the parish, you should immediately notify the top leadership of the parish, the parish's attorney if there is one (if there isn't, there should be), and your own personal attorney, as appropriate. The interesting thing you are about to discover at this time is what it means and feels like to be "in the system." When you are in the system, everything you say or do has potential significance in the larger drama that will be played out in court. What you might say in an offhand remark, for instance, could be conveyed ultimately to a hostile attorney who will be

112

cross-examining you. You will notice that any earlier inclination to spontaneity in thought, word, or deed will have to be checked; you will have to practice diligence, guardedness, and overall caution. Though you may feel like you are becoming paranoid, you are actually only responding appropriately to reality, because you feel as if somebody out there *is* actually trying to hurt you.

The lay leadership and the parish's legal resource are there to support you in an appropriate way, and they are there, of course, to protect the parish as well. Despite any countervailing clericalist notions in your head, the parish as a whole is the community of God's people, and they have a right to be protected, as you have a duty to assist them in that protection. Fortunate indeed will be the parish and priest whose interests are the same in any litigation. It can be a bit complicated, however, if the presumed best interests of the priest are at odds with those of the parish. In the face of this complication, it would behoove the priest to get his or her own attorney or at least to consult separate counsel before rejecting the notion of separate representation. This is a vital step to take for one's own protection.

Attorney Fees

In the matter of attorneys, most Episcopal parishes and their clergy participate in a liability insurance program through the various dioceses. The insurance coverage normally provides for your legal defense, and usually you are indemnified as well—meaning that any legal judgment against you is covered up to a certain limit. (If you have any doubt about the fact or the extent of your insurance coverage, you should check it out. Also, many ordinary homeowner policies indemnify you for liability.) Usually the insurance company will not indemnify you for any instance of overt, deliberate, or malicious harm that you have caused another.

Insurance Coverage

Since the insurance company itself is financing your defense, it usually has the right to choose the attorney who will defend you (or, if it seems appropriate, defend the parish). You may be able to challenge their selection successfully if you want a different lawyer, particularly if the company raises some question about coverage. But you cannot count upon doing so. They pay, so they get their way.

Related to insurance company prerogatives is the right they have to settle out of court. This can be a disheartening discovery for clergy, since they may make the erroneous assumption that, if a certain case is settled out of court, there is probably some culpability on the part of the party being sued. A related reason that out-of-court settlements are rankling is that one never gets the chance to prove one's innocence. There is a certain guilt by innuendo that occurs in a settlement. Still another reason for upset is one's recognition that insurance companies (remember, they are the ones who pay) will settle almost exclusively on the financial ground that it is cheaper for them to do so than to litigate. In other words, settlements occur for financial reasons, not because anybody is liable, partly liable, or free of liability.

People who file lawsuits frequently know all this, and it makes the rhetoric and accusations accompanying such a lawsuit rather beside the point. The real issue in these cases is akin to blackmail: Give us some money (an out-of-court settlement) or we will litigate, and remember that the cost of protracted litigation, with depositions, expert witnesses, attorneys' fees, and the like, may be more expensive than a modest settlement. Most insurance companies, when faced with economics such as this, will settle.

Communications

When a parish is in turmoil because of litigation, the lay leaders of the congregation can perform the important function of listening and interpreting. Maintaining the integrity and cohesiveness of a parish entails being aware of the concerns of the membership, and it entails conveying the facts carefully. Members of the vestry can be deployed as listeners and interpreters, as can the heads of other church groups. Your involvement with this effort must be careful so as to avoid even the appearance of partisanship. The basic facts, however, will need to be conveyed to those who want or need to know them. If confidentiality is not an issue, this can be done fairly, honestly, and discreetly. This is necessary since stewardship of the institution means anticipating unnecessary damage arising from false information, rumor, or gossip. One need not be unduly paranoid in anticipating problems in this area; neither should one be unduly naive. If confidentiality is a factor in the litigation, you will be limited in anything you can say.

In our time of trouble, some lay leaders and I met regularly on Saturday mornings for an hour with interested parishioners who wanted to be kept informed or who otherwise had questions. (There was never any threat to our parish because of allegations against me or the vestry, but I felt it was important to offer the opportunity for people to talk and listen to one another.)

We also sent a simple letter from our attorney to the church's membership when newspaper and television publicity was heaviest, stating the basic facts, denying the allegations against us, and announcing an informal meeting (with refreshments) for a briefing on the matter. Events taking place during this time were not personally worrisome because I felt that the church lay leaders and I had behaved correctly and considerately each step of the way. I knew, too, that we had some personal credibility and that we had the goodwill of the parish. Therefore, getting the facts out appropriately seemed a technical matter of opening up the right channels of communication.

Parish Management

It is sometimes wise, in circumstances involving litigation, to form a "management committee" to handle the day-to-day aspects of litigation-related business. This leaves the clergy more or less free to carry on their normal routines. We formed a management committee consisting of the parish wardens and the parish attorney. The committee's duties included responding to legal matters, such as gathering information, testimony, and evidence that would protect the church. But the most time-consuming (and to me the most personally helpful) task was our attorney's handling of media inquiries. We all agreed that talking to the media ran a serious risk of increasing the attention given to our situation. Further, it could cause us to appear unduly hostile to the person attacking us. Most of all we thought that getting into a "he said, she said" sort of media drama was undignified. There was the obvious complication, too, that what would be found privileged was still being adjudicated or at least reviewed. All phone calls to the church from media people were diverted to the parish's attorney, William Ibershoff, who did a wonderful job of handling them. (When Ibershoff told them the facts of the case, it became just another garden variety embezzlement, a nonstory.)

Publicity

A few more remarks about publicity. Churches or clergy involved either in criminal or civil litigation have the potential for a usable story. A priest should not be surprised at this, nor surprised at the media feeding frenzy that can occur if the allegations involving a priest are truly sensational. Media people are interested in stories. Telling stories is how they make their living. Getting a fantastic story on a national wire service must be enormously rewarding. National attention seems to be the name of the game, no matter what field one is in, and the truth is not always the presiding consideration. (Anyone who reads the tabloids at the supermarket knows what I mean. The headline "Frozen Chicken Comes Back to Life!!!!" is perhaps only an extreme example of what seems to sell papers these days. But not all media people are like tabloid writers, any more than that all clergy are like Jim Bakker.)

If we assume that media people are interested in selling stories at least as much as they are interested in the truth, then it is common sense to recognize that anything you say to a media person *can* be placed, and probably *will* be placed, within the context of *their* story not *yours*. In fact, often the only way to ensure getting your version of what happened into the media is to purchase an advertisement.

The sad thing is that, in selling a story, a media person can be protected from a libel lawsuit by using words like *alleged* and by avoiding the appearance of malice; they can then say pretty much what they like about you if you are a public figure, as clergy frequently are. If you feel terrified of people's misunderstanding when they read your name with, say, "Priest allegedly violated this" or "Priest accused of that," then your horror is entirely reasonable. Those who know you will remember that you were accused of this or that terrible deed, and the accusation or allegation itself will in some way be associated with you for some time thereafter. (Those who don't know you will think, "This person is a real jerk," but they won't remember who you are fifteen minutes later.) That you didn't do anything wrong will be beside the point. The media have a terrific capacity to add dash and color to your lackluster life, simply because someone accuses, and they tell a story. Should it be otherwise? Probably. But I do believe in the freedom of the press and in open society, and so perhaps taking one's lumps in the media now and then is just a part of life, like an occasional cockroach in the spaghetti.[7]

The point is to be careful. People unaccustomed to dealing with the media will be surprised at the force of their own demonic need to talk, even when in their right minds they know they really should say nothing. The attorney for your side should handle all media contacts, and you should adopt an ironclad rule of silence. I offer one last example of the dangers of talking even to friendly media. What this example shows is by no means unique to the particular publication. I choose it as one of countless examples because it is a journal familiar to many Episcopalians.

Many Episcopal Church people will grant that the publication known as the *Living Church* would in all likelihood be favorable to the bishop and the clergy of the Episcopal Diocese of Fond du Lac. Both this publication and the Fond du Lac diocese are located in Wisconsin, and both tend to be supportive of the same issues and concerns. But occasionally not.

First, let me remind you that any of us can be accused of anything, by anyone, at any time. Likewise, we can be sued by anyone willing to pay a filing fee (around $100, let's say). That we are always and everywhere vulnerable to an accusation means that we live pretty much at each other's mercy. The presence of the media does not change this basic fact; the media does, however, magnify the danger to reputation even when the particular media instrument is apparently friendly. I purposely omit mention of the priest's name and alleged crime in quoting this from a portion of a news piece in the February 26, 1989, *Living Church,* which appeared before any report of a trial or conviction: "The Rt. Rev. William Stevens, Bishop of Fond du Lac, stated that he in no way obstructed (investigative) moves against Fr. S——. 'We are cooperating fully with public authorities,' Bishop Stevens told the *Living Church,* 'and are providing all possible rehabilitative treatment for this man, as well as pastoral care for the other individuals.' "[8]

Now my claim. First, the priest in question really ought to be presumed innocent until proven guilty. Second, Bishop Stevens's remarks make it seem, at the very least, that the bishop thinks the priest is culpable of something. Third, many, perhaps most, readers of the news article would assume that the priest is guilty. Fourth, Bishop Stevens's remarks to the *Living Church* are themselves contributory to the appearance of the priest's guilt. And fifth, the impression of guilt has now been disseminated throughout the entire Episcopal Church in the U.S. by the *Living Church.* In truth, based upon the February 26, 1989, article, I do not know whether the priest is guilty of anything, and you don't know that either. We have jury trials in this country to adjudicate such things. Here, however, a bishop talked to the media—friendly media at that—and at the very least the priest's life will never be the same, regardless of what he did or did not do.[9] The net effect is guilty-as-charged journalism.

Keeping One's Own Initiative in Ministry

The issues involved in litigation have a tendency to become all-consuming. Insofar as possible, you should cleave to your ordinary initiative in carrying out your ministry. Most of us went into this profession because we wanted to serve God by serving the Church. This entails the usual business of counseling, marrying, burying, baptizing, preaching, teaching, visiting the sick, and so on. The distraction of litigation is mainly in the time you waste worrying. (My friend Al used to tell me to turn on my "forgetter" —good advice, but also a bit easier said than done, as he knew.) What we can do, though, is to be faithful to our regular appointments, letting God, the people, and their needs command us, doing the best we can in the usual round of our activities.

I've long been taken by a statement of Jürgen Moltmann, one of my favorite theologians, who said this in *Theology of Play:*

> What is the use of God and for what is faith useful? We do not believe freely because it helps us spiritually. We do not pray freely if need has taught us to pray. We do not go to church because it may be to our advantage. We do not properly study theology because it may come in handy later on. We believe insofar as we confront the believable. We pray because it is the privilege of the liberated to talk with God. We go to church because it is a joy to do so when the service is enjoyable. We study theology properly because we are curious and find pleasure in the subject.[10]

That seems quite straightforward and commonsensical. Our job is in large part to create and sustain a climate as inviting as the one Moltmann describes. Accomplishing that is worth one's deepest commitments! Introducing elements of litigation or any peripheral issues into the usual church contexts will not help to achieve it. Try not to let your preaching be diverted by any litigation issues. We do our best ministry when we attend to God, and that sometimes requires a certain commitment of heart, mind, and will. So we just *do* it!

Handling the Psychological Implications of Litigation

The Community of Lawsuit Victims

One of the best and clearest statements about what it feels like to be sued was written by Sara C. Charles, M.D., who was sued for medical malpractice. In her splendid 1985 book *Defendant,* she writes this:

> My first feelings after being charged with medical malpractice were of being utterly alone. Suddenly I felt isolated from my colleagues and patients. Since then I have learned . . . that this feeling of aloneness is not at all unusual, that every physician accused of being negligent has a similar reaction. I also understand that what I experienced during the five-year span of my own case—that it swallowed up my life completely, demanded constant attention and study, multiplied tensions and strain, generated a pattern of broken sleep and anxiety because I felt my integrity as a person and as a physician had been damaged and might be permanently lost—are the common reactions of most doctors accused of negligence. . . .
>
> Doctors not only feel ashamed of practicing medicine defensively, they also feel chagrin and regret that the specter of litigation hovers in the background of their relationships with their patients. What most doctors identify as essential to good medicine, healthy and open relationships with those they treat, is now shadowed with hesitation and uncertainty.[11]

In general, clergy are not as apt to feel as alone as physicians, since the clergy are more immediately a part of a community of people, namely the Church. Although I did not experience these symptoms to the same degree as Dr. Charles, I did experience them. Her book was a support to me for the same reason that phone calls from various physicians were a support: I knew others had gone through this sort of thing and some were probably going through it at the same time I was. You discover an informal "club" of people who have been subjected to lawsuits, and you eventually take a perverse satisfaction in thinking that, after all, only the *most* important and interesting people become part of this club! I have a friend who owns the Golden Nugget Casinos in Las Vegas and Atlantic City. He meant to speak soothing words to me, saying, "A $5 million suit against you? A piddling thing like that—it would never get to my desk. I'd never even see it." I tried to get the whole thing in his perspective, though not entirely successfully.

The Frustration of Wasted Time

Worrying about litigation is just wasted time. Nothing good comes from it, yet you worry anyway. It distracts you. You try thinking about Mrs. Smith, whose child is very sick, and you are fully convinced that in contrast to her predicament, yours is nothing, absolutely nothing. This solution lasts about ten minutes, maybe fifteen. You think about Mr. Brown, who is facing a divorce that he does not want. You know his situation is ten times more dire than yours, but that still doesn't solve your problem, though it helps a little. It's just a bad time, an energy sink. The preoccupation with it, and your recognition at the rational level that the whole thing is absurd from start to finish, top to bottom, still doesn't ever completely distract you from this ridiculous thing. Whatever constitutes the creative thinking in you, whatever enables you to put a touch of excellence on your main interests, tends to be dysfunctional. You lose a certain creative quality and a bit of creative energy, and there's not much you can do about it. In this sense the experience is somewhat similar to the distractions and preoccupations that characterize the grieving process.

Naming the Demon of Inanity

I've always been an avid reader, and I found a phrase in a book review some years ago that stuck in my mind as if glued there. I don't recall the review or the book being reviewed, but I'll never forget this phrase: "the wild and merciless power of inanity." Marvelous! The craziness of life, the inanity of it, is confounding and daunting; then you understand that there *is* a power of inanity in the world. You get hold of a "metaphysic" that enables you to organize the chaos of things in some way: Things *feel* insane and inane because they *are* insane and inane! Eureka!

I have decided that the power of inanity is both wild and merciless and that when you are afflicted by it there's not much you can do except wait for it to end. To pass the time of inanity, I learned not only to appreciate but actually to need daily doses of *The Good Soldier Svejk*.[12] Svejk is a wonderfully inane figure— or is he really the smartest?—in a world gone mad. He became one of my closest friends when the lawsuit was going on. I commend him to you!

Reputation

Your mind tells you not to worry about what other people think about you as a result of allegations against you in the media. Your mind recognizes that you are being much too egocentric when you worry about these things. You know you can't control what others think about you anyway. You know that those who remember your name know you personally, but knowing you personally means knowing you wouldn't do what you are accused of doing. Your mind tells you that the only people who would

120

believe fantastical allegations of the sort hurled at you are those people who will believe in UFOs and extrasensory perception, and who cares about *what* "those people" think? Et cetera, et cetera. But the fact of the matter is that you do care what they think. You discover that a person's reputation is truly a part of his or her basic self, so much so that if your reputation is smeared, *you* are smeared. The great philosopher William James said, "In its widest possible sense . . . a man's self is the sum total of all that he can call his, not only his body and his psychic powers, but his clothes and his house, his wife and children, his ancestors and friends, his reputation. . . ."[13]

Something else happens to you during all this that you recognize as very important, very valuable, immensely useful. It has to do with your understanding, deep down, perhaps deeper than your ability to frame it in words, that actually you *can* live without the understanding or approbation of others. Mind you, you do not prefer to *have* to be so psychologically self-sufficient, but there is a certain exhilaration (I don't know another word for it) that goes with standing firmly on what you know is true. These things get written about, either as they pertain to people of great individual courage or as they pertain to willful and arrogant maniacs. (Since you are not likely to have the perspective to make an accurate judgment concerning the category in which you belong, you might as well place yourself with the saints.)

The Frequent Reminder Phenomenon

Being the subject of media reports presents its hazards. The journalist who reported the filing of a $5 million lawsuit against me was lucky enough to have her story picked up by the Associated Press. Large headlines on page 12A of the August 6, 1985, *San Jose Mercury News* (which broke the story) blared, "Woman sues after priest tells cops of confession."[14] The writer cast her yarn in good-guy, bad-guy terms, and these were frequently reflected in other papers around the country. "Instead of giving absolution, the priest went to the police," said the San Jose paper. A priest I've never met in my life was quoted: Rankin "is one of these very relaxed priests. He's relaxed until he hears what she has to say." The climax of the tale came when the reporter, citing this priest as her source, said, "By listening to [the] confession and later turning her in . . . Rankin violated the absolute secret seal of confession." Bingo! Violated the absolute secret seal of confession! And what kind of priest would do that? Ann Landers

121

answered this question for a correspondent who swallowed the story and wrote her about it: A bad apple! That's what kind![15]

Once the media start spreading reports of your scurrilous character, you will get interesting messages from individuals you don't know. These messages are usually anonymous, which has the wonderful benefit of removing any temptation you feel to send *them* a message or two. I think just now of the devout woman of sincere Christian conviction who called my office one night and told the answering machine, "That rector ought to be crucified! And I'm a Christian, too! From Arizona!" Then there was the unsigned letter from New Jersey threatening my life. And the letter from an Episcopal clergy person in Atlanta who got me mixed up somehow with the ecumenical movement, which he didn't like *either*. I mention all this chiefly as a caveat that there will be constant reminders over the phone and in the mail that some folks out there just don't get things. I generally look forward to opening my mail, but for a while I was getting phobic about it. Even though I didn't receive that much hate mail, a little of this goes a long way!

Distancing Yourself From What You Represent to Your Enemies

You have to be prepared for the fact that somebody out there might really hate you, might really want you dead. This comes as a shock, actually, even though you thought you were old enough by now to have accepted that such sentiments do exist in people. You shouldn't, for all that, take someone else's wish for your harm as a personal matter. It's their mom or dad or life they really hate. You symbolize something to them that is beyond your capacity to control. Instead, think of yourself as incidental to the main problem. Think of yourself as one of the anonymous soldiers in the Trojan War, which like most wars brought into conflict people who had nothing against each other "personally." Think of yourself as simply a target of opportunity for someone with a huge ego problem. Consider this vignette, truly rich in meaning:

> "And were you pleased?" They asked Helen in Hell.
> "Pleased?" answered she, "when all Troy's towers fell;
> And dead were Priam's sons, and lost his throne?
> And such a war was fought as none had known;
> And even the gods took part; and all because of me
>   alone! Pleased?
>   I should say I was!"[16]

So you see, much of what happens to you doesn't have to do with you *personally.* You are just a sad sack in the wrong place at the wrong time.

Self-Control

You might think that with lawyers trying to trip you up, ruin your reputation, and make you look like an idiot, you ought not to submit to malicious impulses of your own. In this you would be correct. One false move on your part and you could be in deep trouble. You discover in an urgent way that the only person who can really hurt you is yourself. And from this insight comes the next, which is that of Martin Luther King and others, concerning the crucial importance of not hating them that hate you. You can see and feel how the wisdom of this is not only idealistic, it is supremely practical. It will be a constant battle, however. Your true feelings will at times come close to those of the novelist Joseph Wambaugh, who once told fellow-writer Janet Malcolm,

"My first nonfiction book, *The Onion Field,* brought me three lawsuits. One of them lasted twelve years. Think of that. Children grow up. Think of how many nights I saw at 3 a.m. . . . These contingency lawyers—they're like garden slugs and bollweevils. You can't get rid of them. Where is Agent Orange when we really need it?"[17]

A thinking person must commend Wambaugh both for his humanity and his candor. A party to litigation, however, must hold cards like these close to the chest.

About Hysteria

I have to pass along this nugget from Gennaro Anguilo, a Boston mob chief who made this comment while unknowingly being bugged by the FBI: "When a man assumes leadership he forfeits the right to mercy."[18] If you are the rector of a parish and are targeted for a lawsuit, bear in mind that you are being paid to endure this little headache; it goes with the territory. You should understand that others expect you to handle it. No histrionics, please, no sniveling. Just handle it. And one of the more feckless things you could do would be to use your present misfortune as a plea for sympathy from people who already dislike you. Likely, they believe you deserve what you are getting. For better or worse—and I believe *much* for the better—your own private struggle is actually of little interest to others. This is as it should be; it reminds you to get your problem in perspective.

123

Avoiding "Defensive Ministry"

I'd say the most important thing is not to fall into the "defensive ministry" trap. I have been asked what I would have done differently in order to avoid the uproar that broke out around me in 1984. My answer has been, "Nothing." We are in this profession because we care about people, and so we take risks for them now and again. The only way I could have avoided that ridiculous and ultimately impotent lawsuit would have been to refuse to try to help the person who ended up suing me. But that would have been callous and entirely too defensive. Maybe I'll get sued again some day. I hope not. But if I do, it might as well be because I offered to help someone, took someone's need seriously. A risk of that sort is far less dangerous, spiritually speaking, than becoming suspicious of people.

In Court: During a Trial

Preliminary Hearing

I said earlier that in anticipation of a court appearance, clergy should keep carefully written records, bearing in mind that these may need to be explained or possibly defended under hostile cross-examination. I have indicated the importance of notifying the bishop and diocesan chancellor as soon as you discover that litigation is pending. It goes without saying that you should not have given even the appearance of harboring malice or vindictive feelings toward your antagonist. You will have obtained competent legal counsel and assured yourself that he or she is skilled in the civil law and also in any aspect of church law that may have significance for your case.

If you are an even remotely important figure in any criminal litigation, you will most likely be involved in a preliminary hearing, perhaps as a witness or, God forbid, as a defendant. The purpose of a preliminary hearing is to enable a judge to decide whether there is sufficient reason to believe a crime has been committed and enough evidence exists in admissible form to enable a trial to take place. This hearing will look to you like the trial itself, which is not a bad thing, because you can think of it as being a dress rehearsal. Depending upon your role, the issues, and circumstances, any and every attempt to challenge, undermine, or discredit your testimony may be made at this time; in the months that pass between now and the actual trial, you can devise ways to strengthen your presentation.

If you are involved in a civil action in some way, you will probably be required to give statements in the form of depositions. These are done in the presence of a stenographer, your attorney, and the attorney for the other party. The purpose of depositions is to get at the facts in preliminary, documented testimony.

Giving Testimony

At the trial itself you will be cross-examined. You will have the advantage of having faced the attorney before; he or she, however, will have the larger advantage of knowing your testimony from the preliminary hearing. Chances are that he or she will try to trap you on the basis of what you said then. One way to accomplish this is to try to "impeach" your testimony, which is to say, try to have you contradict what you said before. Your best defense against this possibility is (1) always tell the truth and (2) review your copy of the hearing transcript, which reports exactly what you said.

I truly believe that the most wonderful right one can have in giving testimony is the right to explain one's answers. If you are fully aware of this, you can adopt a more relaxed attitude than you might otherwise be inclined to take. But you will also discover an uneasy feeling that you are only a pawn in a larger battle in which the major actors are the various attorneys. Each seems to be in possession of his or her own master strategy; each seems to know where he or she wants to end up and precisely how they intend to get there. You may well feel that you are a friendly pawn being deployed by one of them and that to the other you are an obstacle to be removed. You are not likely to know exactly how you fit into the overarching apocalyptic struggle, either because it is too complicated and time-consuming for a friendly attorney to explain or (always a possibility) because the attorney doesn't exactly know. There will be few moments, in fact, when you will be *unaware* that you are only a pawn, and this can be quite disconcerting. (Now you know how lay people feel when they get lost in the liturgy!) In the case of a civil trial, the overall objective of your attorney, you can be sure, is to persuade the jury that your side is the "good" side and the other side is "bad." The other side has a comparable objective! Juries, I'm told, are pretty good at spotting phonies and liars, so for heaven's sake, be yourself.

The Privilege

Claiming the clergy-communicant privilege is a rather simple thing to do, actually. It's done by just doing it. If or when you are questioned as to *why* you think you can validly assert the privilege, your answer should be along this line: "With utmost respect, your honor, even though I would otherwise like to answer that question, I find I simply cannot. I am bound to keep a confidence." Most judges will be favorably disposed to allow you to claim the privilege. But judges vary, and circumstances do, too. Your attorney will be your best resource on what to do, how to do it, and what to expect from the judge.

Your Professional Role

In general, it is always good to remember that you are a professional clergy person. This means that, in offering testimony, your objective is not to prosecute people or otherwise bring down harm upon them. Rather, it is simply to tell the truth. If another person has gotten him or herself into a tight spot—perhaps as the defendant in a criminal trial—that is not your sole or perhaps even overriding responsibility, and usually you are not responsible for rescuing them. You are certainly concerned about anyone in trouble; but by the time things have gotten to the trial stage there is precious little you can do by way of rescue.

If you are the defendant—say, in a civil malpractice suit—your demeanor should be one of dignity, forthcoming honesty, and sincerity. Coming across as unjustly accused, righteously indignant, precious, unctious, or whatever, would not be to your advantage. Judges and juries are there to try to figure out what the facts are and what rules of law appropriately apply to them. Your job is *simply* to tell the truth.

The Outcome of a Trial

When it's all over, if your side prevails you may be inclined to gloat, and if your side loses, to despair. Don't do either. If you lose, there is always the possibility of an appeal. In either case, you should continue to do what you have presumably been trying to do all along, which is to serve God by serving God's people to the best of your ability. Even in the worst possible scenario, your having failed in the legal context places you in the same camp as the Lord Jesus, though I wouldn't want to push that analogy too far. No matter what has happened, we should remember that we get involved with people as ministers, trying to do the best we can and occasionally having precious little control over the forces that swirl all around us. We are called to risk, to love even them that revile us, and to keep faith with God, with God's entire community, and with ourselves. Nothing is guaranteed. That is why faith is necessary and why good faith means persevering in love, regardless.

Afterword:

Some Last Thoughts

I am uncomfortable with setting forth any apparently conclusive statement when the subject is people, ministry, or life. God is not finished with any of us, as we have been told. Clergy know better than they might like that there will be surprises for them, new situations, unique stories, unusual needs, problems, and challenges—this is what contributes to the excitement and richness of our profession. The unpredictability of all that we face means that conclusive or definitive approaches will sometimes be beside the point. Indeed, if we try to anticipate each new exigency with a prefabricated rule, we have begun to abandon our own humanity; the ministry could then as easily be done by computer.

Yet we do take seriously the time-honored principles that have repeatedly enabled both God and humankind to be served appropriately. The social ethics question, "What should be done?" (*generally*) must be answered in a categorical way: confidences should be kept. Of course! But then there are singular circumstances in which a different sort of question arises: "Yes, confidences should be kept, generally, but now, faced with the uniqueness of this present situation, what should I do?"

The poets seem to be especially alert to the subtleties of life and people. John Keats had a way of stating his respect for the ambiguities of life and the way in which these caused a resistance in him to definitive formulations. In a December 22, 1817, letter to his brothers Thomas and George, the poet described the principle of "negative capability," meant to state his capacity to identify with different, sometimes contradictory, realities without simultaneously lusting after a precise, definitive resolution or a fully satisfying choice between them. One who possesses negative capability will be able to hold different views simultaneously, and tentatively; things are not simplistically definitive.

For Keats, Shakespeare was the master of this principle. Shakespeare's ability to develop so fully all his various characters bespoke his respect for the contradictions, the mystery, ambiguities, and tentativeness that are plainly there in life. Shakespeare's characters could never be drawn simply, because no human life is simple; Shakespeare was not a cartoonist. To be conscious of these things, as he was, means that we frequently give only tentative force to our assessments of people, decision dilemmas, and events in general. Here is a basis for our commonsensical aversion to legalism and other idolatries. Paul Tillich was a theological mentor along this line, chiefly by way of his "Protestant principle," an insistence that we not assign infinite value to the finite.

I think of Keats's principle of negative capability and Tillich's Protestant principle when I reflect upon the tricky business of honoring other people, self, God, community, truth, justice, love—and confidences! Keats's insight needs to be acknowledged if we are to be honest about what we sometimes feel—sometimes *should* feel—when we are required to make commitments and decisions in complex situations. I believe we are more fully human when we do feel the ambiguity and paradox of complex circumstances and when we acknowledge, at least to ourselves, what we feel. Our acknowledgment may enable us to avoid mesmerization in our feelings; we may instead be able to come to terms more deliberately with decisions that must be made.

All this I have said before: *sometimes* our simple rules, our pledges of confidentiality, do not take adequate account of the situation before us. Nor, perhaps, do they allow us to exercise our fuller humanity, which we know on religious grounds is based in love and justice. There is sometimes no right, definitive, or even safe path down which we can safely travel in our dealings with people and their complex problems in this surprising and mysterious world. If Keats had written an ethics textbook on confidentiality, he might have urged us to be people of principle, people accepting a prima facie duty to keep confidences. But I also think he would have commended to us the sensibility he valued so importantly and described so well as the principle of negative capability. (A physician friend, whom I admire both as a physician and as a human being, told me he had always based his diagnosis upon the best medical insights *and* the principle of negative capability. For my money, clergy should do similarly.)

Most clergy know very well that there is plenty of work to do in simply running a parish; sometimes doing what's right can open an enormous can of worms. For example, if a priest has his or her hands more than full in trying to raise money for the operating budget, recruit church school teachers, counsel the divorcing, support the dying, and do all the other duties, then to report an abused kid—when the alternative is simply to ignore the situation—can seem beyond one's ability. The mind says such a thing should be done. The body, however, resists.

Swinging the mind into alignment with the intransigent body is sometimes infinitely easier than doing it the other way around. We rationalize. Good intentions and larger purposes abound. "Keeping the larger picture in focus," "being pastoral," and (behold!) "honoring the duty to keep a confidence" frequently suffice. Values such as those enshrined in these phrases are intrinsically commendable, certainly, but the political uses of the phrases themselves may not be. One's chief aim might be only to keep one's tasks, and life, amiably smooth; but there can be no particular virtue in such an endeavor. Doing what love or justice requires may threaten my convenience, but accepting the claims of love and justice is what one should do when one becomes a Christian.

I propose that seminary courses or clergy conferences or clergy associations might profitably undertake training in some of the thorny problems of confidentiality. An attorney skilled in civil and church law might be a useful resource. (I have discovered, though, that not all attorneys who claim to be competent in church law and civil law may be competent in both, or in either.) Anyway, my experience is that clergy tend to need, and tend to be very appreciative of, training in the ethics and law of confidentiality.

Another proposal is that dioceses impanel a group of clergy, attorneys, laity, and others as an ongoing ethics committee. Such a committee could be of help to the bishop and chancelor, as well as to parish clergy and lay leaders. Lawyers, physicians, and hospitals, after all, have professional standards review bodies and ethics committees of one sort or another. Why not have the same for clergy and the church? The absence of clear ethical codes argues for some ongoing resource of this sort. The various hospital ethics committees have developed very effective procedures for undertaking their work (including ways of safeguarding confidentiality in their ethical deliberations). There may be much that could be applied usefully to church ethics committees at the diocesan level.

Before attempting a summary statement, I note that at different locations in this book I make different suggestions, or imply certain solutions, to the various problems addressed in it. To recapitulate those would be tiresome. I do think one point is worth making again, however, because it is truly important. This is that precisely because there are no guaranteed, comprehensive rules to follow that will always ensure we have done the right and the good, we should always treat people with kindness and respect. We should bring to bear a thoughtful competence upon their plight, whatever it might be. We ought to do the best we can to take people's needs seriously, and, subject to common sense, we ought even to take risks for them. We ought to take risks also for their children and for any others whom our people (once in a great while, deliberately or not) might have hurt or might be about to hurt. As Christians we are not here only to honor and comply with those who pay the bills at the dear old church. The scope of our concern is broader and different. Jesus broke open the boundaries of our narrow concern when he spoke of the neighborhood of his ministry this way: *Be* a neighbor to people in need, regardless of their proximity, as the Samaritan was a neighbor to the Jew who was hurt.

We should do the caring thing, the rightful thing, the thing that respects the humanity of the other, the self, and the reality of God. We should keep our word, honor confidences, tell the truth, be people of moral principle, yes. And we should also respect the mystery of things, the surprises, which place in question, now and then, the principled ways in which we have tried to approach people and situations. What love and justice require will not always be clear. Still, we walk by faith. When I consider very complex situations, I grow more aware of another element that should be added when applying principles or rules to cases. I am aware of how vague this might seem and how possibly anomic. But I admit to being guided in tough dilemmas by my imagining what the Galilean would do in them.

Perhaps imagining things in this way helps us root our moral life in our religious life. We may become better able to live and decide in ways that are both morally principled and (possibly) in-spirited by that great life. Given the enormous complexities of the world these days, which require of us the most searching and conscientious decisions, to be moral and spiritually conscientious in this dual way may be just right. *How* one might speak adequately of the spirit of Jesus in a decision-making context would be the subject of another book. I end this one stating my belief that Jesus evidently recognized the importance of moral principles, but he also indicated that these were made for humankind, rather than the other way around. And there are indications that he departed from the conventions of his time and place when doing so was needed in order to help others. We live by principles, yes; but even more we live within the generous spirit of his life.

Notes

Introduction

1. Marie M. Fortune, *Is Nothing Sacred?* (San Francisco: Harper & Row, 1989), presents a powerful case for the development of a professional ethic for clergy. She also urges that the churches assign the highest priority to specifying a clear and fair adjudication process when clergy have been accused of professional misconduct. Her central concern is with alleged or real sexual misconduct in clergy pastoral contexts, rather than with issues of confidentiality specifically. Her book is a most impressive contribution.

Chapter 1. The Ethos of the Church and the Ethics of Its Clergy

1. Lin Yutang, "Why I Came Back to Christianity," *Presbyterian Life*, 15 April 1959. Reprinted in Hugh T. Kerr and John M. Mulder, eds., *Conversions* (Grand Rapids: Eerdmans, 1983), 205–29.
2. Ibid., 208.
3. Ibid., 209.
4. Clifton Fadiman, ed., *The Little, Brown Book of Anecdotes* (Boston: Little, Brown, 1985), 251.
5. Joseph Conrad, "The Return," in *Tales of Unrest* (1902). Quoted in John Bartlett, *Familiar Quotations.* (Boston: Little, Brown, 1980), 683.
6. Kirkpatrick Sale, *Nation*, 14 March 1987, 323.
7. Martin E. Marty, "But Who's Counting?" *Christian Century*, 6–13 July 1988, 655. Quoting David B. Barrett, *World Christian Encyclopedia* (Oxford University Press, 1982), as updated annually in *International Bulletin of Missionary Research*.
8. Joseph Brodsky, "A Commencement Address," *New York Review of Books*, 16 August 1984, 7.
9. Joseph Heller, *God Knows* (New York: Knopf, 1984), 294.

10. Ernest Hemingway, "A Writer's Job is to Tell the Truth," in *Men at War*, ed. Ernest Hemingway (New York: Bramhall House, 1943), xiii.
11. After William E. Hulme, *Pastoral Care and Counseling* (Minneapolis: Augsburg, 1981), 9.
12. Eugene Kennedy, *On Becoming a Counselor: A Basic Guide for Non-Professional Counselors* (New York: Continuum, 1977).
13. Harry Bone, "The Field of Counseling," introduction to Rollo May, *The Art of Counseling* (New York and Nashville: Abingdon, 1967), 15–17.
14. John Cobb, *Theology and Pastoral Care* (Philadelphia: Fortress, 1977).
15. Ibid., 2.

Chapter 2. The Confession

1. See, for example, Philippe Delhaye, *Pastoral Treatment of Sin* trans. Charles Schaldenbrand et al. (New York: Desclee, 1968); and Delhaye, *The Christian Conscience*, trans. Charles U. Quinn (New York: Desclee, 1968).
2. K.N.T. newswire in the Marin County, California, *Independent Journal*, 13 June 1986.
3. Reedy's comments are reported in the same K.N.T. wire as above.
4. Francis G. Belton, *A Manual for Confessors* (London: Mowbray, 1949); Kenneth Ross, *Hearing Confession* (London: SPCK, 1974); Martin L. Smith, *Reconciliation: Preparing for Confession in the Episcopal Church* (Boston: Cowley, 1985). Smith is more rigid than I am, it appears, on the "seal." See also Bernard Poschmann, *Penance and the Anointing of the Sick* (New York: Herder, 1964); Tad Guzie, *What a Modern Catholic Believes about Confession* (Chicago: Thomas More, 1974); Tad Guzie and John McIlhon, *The Forgiveness of Sin* (Chicago: Thomas More, 1979); Robert J. Kennedy, ed., *Reconciliation: The Continuing Agenda* (Collegeville MN: Liturgical Press, 1987).
5. Virgilius Ferm, ed., *The Encyclopedia of Religion* (Secaucus, N.J.: Poplar Books, 1987).
6. Ibid., 46.
7. Karl Rahner, "Penance," in *Sacramentum Mundi* (New York: Herder & Herder, 1969), 4:385–99.

8. Avery Dulles, *Models of the Church* (Garden City, N.Y.: Doubleday, 1974), 61.
9. Ferm, *Encyclopedia of Religion*, 46.
10. John E. Booty, "Contrition in Anglican Spirituality," in *Anglican Spirituality*, ed. William Wolf (Wilton, Conn.: Morehouse-Barlow, 1982), 26.
11. Ibid., 27.
12. Ibid., 28.
13. Ibid., 27.
14. Ibid., 29.
15. Ibid., 43.
16. Charles Price and Louis Weil, *Liturgy for Living* (New York: Seabury, 1979), 54.
17. Ibid., 270.
18. Meg Greenfield, *Newsweek*, 15 June 1987, 80.
19. Ferm, *Encyclopedia of Religion*, 2.
20. James F. Childress and John MacQuarrie, eds., *Westminster Dictionary of Christian Ethics* (Philadelphia: Westminster, 1986), 112.
21. Ibid.
22. Quoted in Sissela Bok, *Secrets* (New York: Vintage, 1984), 78.
23. Price and Weil, *Liturgy for Living*, 271.
24. Marion J. Hatchett, *Commentary on the American Prayer Book* (New York: Seabury, 1981).
25. John T. McNeill, *History of the Cure of Souls* (San Francisco: Harper & Row, 1977).
26. McNeill, *History of the Cure of Souls*, 219.
27. J.R.H. Moorman, *A History of the Church in England*, 3rd ed. (London: A. & C. Black, 1986), 225.
28. See Richard S. Nolan, "The Law of the Seal of Confession," in *The Catholic Encyclopedia* 13:656.
29. William Tiemann and John C. Bush, *The Right to Silence: Privileged Clergy Communication and the Law* (Nashville: Abingdon, 1983), 54.
30. Quoted in McNeill, *History of the Cure of Souls*, 226.
31. Ibid., 228.
32. Ibid., 228.
33. John E. Booty, "The English Reformation: A Lively Faith and Sacramental Confession," in *The Anglican Moral Choice*, ed. Paul Elmen, (Wilton, Conn.: Morehouse-Barlow, 1983), 15–32.

34. Ibid., 15.
35. Ibid., 16.
36. Ibid.
37. Ibid., 19.
38. Ibid.
39. Ibid., 20.
40. Ibid., 31–35.
41. Booty, "Contrition in Anglican Spirituality," 25ff.
42. H.R. McAdoo, "Anglican Moral Theology in the 17th Century," in *The Anglican Moral Choice*, ed. Paul Elmen (Wilton, Conn.: Morehouse-Barlow, 1983), 45.
43. Ibid.
44. Martin Thornton, *English Spirituality* (N.p., 1963), 251. Quoted in McAdoo, "Anglican Moral Theology," 48.
45. McAdoo, "Anglican Moral Theology," 48. Emphasis added.
46. McNeill, *History of the Cure of Souls*, 231.
47. Gerald R. Cragg, *The Church and the Age of Reason, 1648–1789* (New York: Penguin, 1977).
48. Ibid., 169.
49. Ibid., 139.
50. Alex Vidler, *The Church in an Age of Revolution: 1789 to the Present Day* (Baltimore: Penguin Books, 1976), 168. See also J.R.H. Moorman, *A History of the Church in England* (Wilton, Conn.: Morehouse-Barlow, 1980), 364.
51. John R.W. Stott, *Confess Your Sins: The Way of Reconciliation* (Philadelphia: Westminster Press, 1964), 84.

Chapter 3. Confession in the Episcopal Church

1. F.L. Cross, ed., *The Oxford Dictionary of the Christian Church*, 2d ed., revised by F.L. Cross and E.A. Livingstone (New York: Oxford University Press, 1979), 1254.
2. Marion J. Hatchett, *Commentary on the American Prayer Book* (New York: Seabury Press 1981), 454.
3. Brice Schratz, "Seal of Confession," in *The Encyclopedia of Religion*, ed. Vergilius Ferm (Secaucus, N.J.: Poplar Books, 1945 and 1987), 698.
4. Francis J. Hall, *The Sacraments* (New York: Longmans, Green, 1921), chap. 7, "Penance."
5. Ibid., 24.
6. Ibid., 242.
7. *Doctrine in the Church of England* (London: SPCK 1938).
8. Ibid., 191.

9. Ibid., 197.
10. *The Canons of the Church of England* (London: SPCK, 1969), 82.
11. Sir William Dale, *The Law of the Parish Church* (London: Butterworth's, 1967).
12. Ibid., 2.
13. Ibid., 5.
14. Ibid., 6.
15. Cited in Raymond Albright, *A History of the Protestant Episcopal Church* (New York: Macmillan, 1964), 127.
16. The complete statement is cited in Leighton Coleman, *The Church in America* (New York: Pott, 1875), 137–40.
17. Albright, *History of the Protestant Episcopal Church*, 129.
18. *The Book of Common Prayer* (New York: Seabury, 1979), 9.
19. Cross, ed., *Oxford Dictionary*, 1207.
20. J.C. Davies, ed., *The Westminster Dictionary of Liturgy and Worship* (Philadelphia: Westminster Press, 1986), 472.
21. John Wall, Jr., *A New Dictionary for Episcopalians* (Minneapolis: Winston Press, 1985).
22. E.A. White and J.A. Dykman, *Annotated Constitution and Canons . . .*, vol. 1 (New York: Seabury Press, 1981).
23. Ibid., 443.
24. Ibid., 445.
25. Albright, *History of the Protestant Episcopal Church*, 285.
26. Quoted in Albright, *History of the Protestant Episcopal Church*, "Landian" is a reference to Bishop Land, the esteemed symbol of Anglo-Catholicism in the English Church of the mid-seventeenth century.
27. Ibid., 181.
28. Ibid., 236.
29. Ibid.
30. Byron D. Stuhlman, *Prayer Book Rubrics Expanded* (New York: Church Hymnal Corporation, 1987), viii.
31. Undated, quoted in Tiemann and Bush, *Right to Silence*, 59.

Chapter 4. Pastoral Counseling

1. Marie M. Fortune, in *Christian Century*, 18–25 June 1986, 582.
2. *Children's Healthcare Is a Legal Duty (CHILD)* (Sioux City, IA, Summer 1988), 1. (Newsletter).
3. Ibid., 14.

4. "Who decides what is confidential?" News item in *Christian Century*, 23 December 1987, 1109.
5. Reported in *Christian Century*, 7 October 1987, 850.
6. Ibid.
7. Bergman, "Is the Cloth Unraveling?" in Malony, Needham, and Southard, *Clergy Malpractice* (Philadelphia: Westminster Press, 1986), 22.
8. *Walter J. Nally et al. v. Grace Community Church*, 253 Cal. Rptr. 97, 763 p. 2d 948.
9. Bernard Witkin, *Summary of California Law*, 10th ed. (1988), Torts, s6, p. 61.
10. (1981) 16 Val. U.L. Rev. 163, 176.
11. *Cantwell v. Connecticut*, 1940, 310 U.S. 296. 303–4, 60 S.Ct. 900, 903, 84 L.Ed. 1213; and other cases.
12. (1982) 455 U.S. 252, 261, 102 S.Ct. 1051, 1057 71 L.Ed. 2d. 127

Chapter 5. Ethics and the Limits of Confidentiality

1. Bok, *Secrets*, 120.
2. Samuel D. Warren and Louis D. Brandeis, "The Right to Privacy," 4 *Harvard Law Review* 193 (1890).
3. 398 U.S. 479 (1967), 350.
4. 410 U.S. 113 (1973), 152.
5. Ibid., 154.
6. Ibid., 152.
7. 97 S.Ct. 869 (1977).
8. Richard F. Hixson, *Privacy in a Public Society: Human Rights in Conflict* (New York: Oxford University Press, 1987).
9. Ibid., 56.
10. Bok, *Secrets*, 121.
11. Ibid., 123.
12. For more concerning a woman's perspective on these issues, see Ann-Janine Morey, "Blaming Women for the Sexually Abusive Male Pastor," *Christian Century*, 5 October 1988, 866–69; and the sources cited therein.
13. Don S. Browning, *The Moral Context of Pastoral Care* (Philadelphia: Westminster Press, 1976).
14. Don S. Browning, *Religious Ethics and Pastoral Care* (Philadelphia: Fortress Press, 1983).
15. Ibid., 10.
16. *Washington Post Health*, 19 April 1988, 6.

17. *Confronting AIDS: Update, 1988* (Washinton: National Academy Press, 1988). No author given.
18. *Report of the Presidential Commission on the Human Immunodeficiency Virus Epidemic* (Washington: U.S. Government Printing Office, 1988).
19. Quoted in Bok, *Secrets*, 128.
20. Morris B. Abram, *New York Times* 31 March 1986.
21. An interesting example of this commonsensical point is the observation once made by a psychoanalyst, Harry Stack Sullivan, I'm told, to the effect that the difference between an experienced analyst and a novice is that the former recognizes a hysteric sooner and runs away faster.

Chapter 6. Professional Ethics and the Law
1. Robert M. Veatch and Sarah T. Fry, *Case Studies in Nursing Ethics* (Philadelphia: Lippincott, 1987), 143.
2. *Gammill v. U.S.*, 727 F.2d 950 (10th Cir. 1984), for instance.
3. Veatch and Fry, *Case Studies in Nursing Ethics*, 142.
4. Dean L. Hummel, Lou C. Talbutt, and M. David Alexander, *Law and Ethics in Counseling* (New York: Van Nostrand Reinhold, 1985).
5. *Roe v. Wade*, 410 U.S. 113, 93 S.Ct. 705, 35 L.Ed. 147 (1973): "The constitution does not explicitly mention any right of privacy."
6. Charles W. Wolfram, *Modern Legal Ethics* (St. Paul: West Publishing, 1986).
7. David Luban, *Lawyers and Justice: An Ethical Study* (Princeton: Princeton University Press, 1988).
8. Ibid., 185.
9. Ibid., xxi.
10. Ibid., 112.
11. Quoted in *Harper's*, June 1984, First page of "Readings."
12. Luban, *Lawyers and Justice*, 127.
13. Wolfram, *Modern Legal Ethics*, 244.
14. Ibid., 247.
15. Ibid.
16. Ibid. 251.
17. Ibid., 268.
18. In re Gray, 123 Ca. App. 3d 614, 176 Cal. Rptr. 721 (1981), and other cases.
19. *Skelton v. Spencer*, 98 Idaho 417, 565 p.2d 1374 (1977).

20. Wolfram, *Modern Legal Ethics*, 281.
21. *U.S. v. Gordon-Nikkar*, 518 F.2d 972, 975 (5th Cir. 1975).
22. In re John Doe Corp. 675 F.2d 482, 491 (2nd Cir. 1982).
23. Luban, *Lawyers and Justice*, 33.
24. Wolfram, *Modern Legal Ethics*, 664; and Luban, *Lawyers and Justice*, 53. *People v. Garrow*, 51 A.D. 2d 814, 379, N.Y.S. 2d 185 (1976).
25. *People v. Belge*, 50 A.D. 2d 1088, 376 N.Y.S. 2d 771 (1975), subsequently affirmed. See note 6 in Wolfram, *Modern Legal Ethics*, 664.
26. A.D. 2d 1088, 376 N.Y.S. 2d 771, 772 (1975).
27. N.Y. St. Bar. Ethics Op. 479 (1978).
28. *Spaulding v. Zimmerman*, 116 NW 2d 704 (1962), appearing in Luban, *Lawyers and Justice*, 149f.
29. All law libraries contain numerous commentaries on the First Amendment.
30. *Cantwell v. Connecticut* (1940) 310 U.S. 296, 303, 60 S.Ct. 900, 84 L.Ed. 1213.
31. *Kedroff v. St. Nicholas Cathedral* (1952) 344 U.S. 94. 120–21, 73 S.Ct. 143, 97 L.Ed. 120.
32. *Kreshik v. St. Nicholas Cathedral* (1960) 363 U.S. 190, 191, 80 S.Ct. 1037, 4 L.Ed. 2d 1140).
33. *Committee for Public Education v. Nyquist* (1973) 413 U.S. 756, 772–73, 93 S.Ct. 2955, 37 L.Ed. 2d 948.
34. See John E. Nowak, Ronald D. Rotunda, and J. Nelson Young, "Freedom of Religion," *Constitutional Law* (1983), 1029–81.
35. *Rankins v. Commission of Professional Competence* (1979) 24 C.3d 167, 177–78, 593 2d 852.
36. *U.S. v. Lee* (1982) 455 U.S. 252, 261, 102 S.Ct. 1051, 1057, 71 L.Ed.2d 1276.
37. Jacob M. Yellin, "The History and Current Status of the Clergy-Penitent Privilege," *Santa Clara Law Review* 23, no. 123 (1983).
38. *II Halsbury's Laws of England*, 4th ed. (1973), paragraph 464; quoted in Yellin, "Clergy-Penitent Privilege," 103.
39. Yellin, "Clergy-Penitent Privilege," 112.
40. California Evidence Code Section 1032.
41. See *In Re Lifshutz* (1970) 2 Cal.3d 415, 428, 467 p.2d 557.
42. Witkin, *California Evidence*, 3rd ed., 1220–22.

43. Roy D. Weinberg, *Confidential and Other Privileged Communication*, Legal Almanac series no. 61 (Dobbs Ferry, N.Y.: Oceana Publications, 1967), 81.
44. William H. Tiemann and John C. Bush, *The Right to Silence: Privileged Clergy Communication and the Law* (Nashville: Abingdon, 1983).
45. Remark of attorney Richard R. Hammar in a news item, quoted in *Church and State*, June 1986, 11.
46. Tiemann and Bush, *Right to Silence*, 85; citing *Simrin v. Simrin*, 43 Calif. Rep. 376. Dist. Ct. App. 1965.
47. Yellin, "Clergy-Penitent Privilege," 95–156.
48. Remark of Leo Pfeffer in a news item, quoted in *Church and State*, June 1986, 11.

Chapter 7. Managing Yourself and Parish under the Impact of Litigation

1. Sissela Bok, *A Strategy for Peace: Human Values and the Threat of War* (New York: Pantheon Books, 1988).
2. Ibid., 47.
3. Ibid., 48.
4. See, for instance, the unpublished D.Min. dissertation of Sue Ellen Westfall, *Developing Downtown Ministry to Homeless Mentally Ill People*. San Francisco Theological Seminary. San Anselmo, CA, 1989.
5. Concerning this point, and the next few, I am borrowing from *Church Risk Management (CRM) News*, Spring 1988, published by the Church Pension Fund, New York, N.Y.
6. Ibid., 1.
7. I've been collecting bits and pieces concerning the ethics of the media. The good things that good media people do are worthy of our highest praise. The less attractive tendencies are worrisome. Anyone interested in the broad subject could read "A Look at the News Media," *Washington Spectator*, 14:4, 15 February 1988; Anthony Lewis, "The Intimidated Press," *New York Review of Books*, 19 January 1989; and Theodor Draper, "Rewriting the Iran-Contra Story," *New York Review of Books*, 19 January 1989.
8. *Living Church*, 26 February 1989, 7.
9. This case took another turn subsequently. Three weeks after its first account of the Fond du Lac situation, *Living Church* printed a four-paragraph follow-up. Its first

paragraph reported the no contest plea of the priest to two counts of second-degree sexual assault. The great bulk of the article (the remaining three paragraphs), however, consisted of protestations that the bishop of Fond du Lac had certainly *not* hindered the local district attorney's investigation of the priest, as some might have erroneously believed. Rather, states the article, various prosecutors actually praised the diocese for its willing assistance in the criminal investigation. The piece closed by citing the bishop's remark that a prosecuting attorney had himself noted that "the diocese did more than it had to" in supporting the investigation of the priest. (*Living Church*, 19 March 1989, 7). From all this we can see the media's usefulness in making clear that Fond du Lac is not the place for miscreant priests *or* any who doubt diocese-police cooperation!

10. Jürgen Moltmann, *Theology of Play*, trans. Reinhard Ulrich (New York: Harper & Row, 1972), 66.
11. Sara C. Charles, M.D., and Eugene Kennedy, *Defendant: A Psychiatrist on Trial for Medical Malpractice* (New York: Free Press, 1985), xiii and xiv.
12. Jaroslav Hasek, *The Good Soldier Svejk* trans. Cecil Parrott, with the original illustrations by Josef Lada (New York: Thomas Crowell, 1974).
13. William James, *The Principles of Psychology* (1890), chap. 10. Quoted in John Bartlett, *Familiar Quotations* (Boston: Little, Brown, 1980), 648.
14. *San Jose Mercury News*, 6 August 1985.
15. Ann Landers, "Bad Apples," *San Francisco Examiner*, 23 March 1986.
16. Lord Dunsany, quoted in John Julius Norwich, *Christmas Crackers* (New York: Penguin, 1982).
17. Janet Malcolm, "The Journalist and The Murderer," *New Yorker*, 20 March 1989, 70.
18. Quoted in *Harper's* magazine, October 1988, 24.